D1302362

**DATE DUE**

# Meditations with Tea

# Meditations with Tea

## PATHS TO INNER PEACE

Diana Rosen

CITADEL PRESS
KENSINGTON PUBLISHING CORP.
WWW.KENSINGTONBOOKS.COM

CITADEL PRESS books are published by

Kensington Publishing Corp.
850 Third Avenue
New York, NY 10022

All Kensington titles, imprints, and distributed lines are available at special quantity discounts for bulk purchases for sales promotions, premiums, fund-raising, educational, or institutional use. Special book excerpts or customized printings can also be created to fit specific needs. For details, write or phone the office of the Kensington special sales manager: Kensington Publishing Corp., 850 Third Avenue, New York, NY 10022, attn: Special Sales Department; phone 1-800-221-2647.

First printing: July 2004

10  9  8  7  6  5  4  3  2

Printed in the United States of America

Library of Congress Control Number: 2004100515

ISBN 0-8065-2616-5

*For the dedicated men and women who plant and harvest,*
*process and package, source and cup,*
*to bring us our meditative cup of tea.*
*And, for the teachers of meditation practices of all types*
*who remind us that fulfillment can surface, even from buried chaos.*
*Thank you.*

# CONTENTS

One should clean out a room in one's home and place only a tea table and a chair in the room with some boiled water and fragrant tea. Afterward, sit comfortably, and allow one's spirit to become tranquil, light, and natural.

—Li Ri Hua, scholar,
Ming dynasty (1368–1644)

# PREFACE: WHY COMBINE MEDITATION WITH TEA?

*Tea is drunk to forget the din of the world.*

—T'ien Yiheng, eighth-century Chinese sage

*T*hank you for picking up this book. It is the first encounter on an incredibly mysterious yet ultimately satisfying journey where we will discover how very true it is that everyone, men and women, must have a treasured space all their own, the pleasure of a cup of tea, and some time to enjoy them both.

For many of us, meditation *is* a cup of tea. Its fragrance can be like the most delicate of spring blooms, its taste like the nectar of the best summer fruit, and it will have its way with our body and mind, soothing, assuring, allowing us to go outside of ourselves and return refreshed and restored.

Meditation has many nuances. For some it is a regimented practice with a goal of what the Japanese call *satori*, the experience of comprehension, or what others refer to as pure enlightenment. At the very least, meditation is a respite, a time to collect our emotions together with our rational self and comfort each part. Meditation is a form of prayer, a communion with God, Spirit, that "something" that we turn to when questions become unanswerable, problems unsolvable, gratitude spills over, joy must be shared.

If you ever take time to sit quietly, pray, wish, wonder, hope, think with intent, you may know ways to meditate. If you daydream, relax, allow your mind to wander and return, providing you with a dip into your inner self that feeds you and quenches you with a nutritious spirit, then you certainly know ways to meditate.

How does tea figure into meditation? The simple act of making tea demands attention outside of yourself. To make tea well is simple to learn and requires water, tea leaves, a cup, and time. You cannot rush the preparation of tea. Too little time and the flavor will not be there. Neglecting the clock and you end with a bitter cup. You cannot drink it quickly, either. Its pleasures are many, requiring only some leisure to appreciate its fragrance, its taste, its warmth, its caress to the body and mind.

Meditation can be the most nourishing of companions and the preparation of and drinking of tea can only accentuate this communion between all that you are and all that you want to be. In this book you will explore some simple yet effective ways of enhancing the meditation experience. They benefit body and soul and mind, require no equipment, expense, or exceptional experience. By inviting the joy of drinking tea to be an integral part of this "small pleasure," tea becomes a conduit that allows peace and harmony to flow within you.

I have been inspired by the maxim of Sen Sôshitsu XV, Grand Tea Master of the Urasenke School, one of the three schools of Japanese tea ceremony (*chanoyu*). Literally translated as "water for tea," *chanoyu*, says Sen Sôshitsu, is a way of serving tea—with pureness of heart—that is a way of life. For decades the venerable tea master has traveled the world to meet with world leaders, to share a bowl of tea, and relate his message of peace. In his most famous book, *Tea Life, Tea Mind*, he writes, "Taking a bowl of green tea in your hands and drinking it, you feel one with nature, and there is peace." From him, and other teachers of tea and meditation, I continue to carve out my own path. What I have learned has been transforming and I trust that it will be, at the very least, intriguing to you.

Several years ago, through a variety of circumstances, I became a house- and pet-sitter. The houses were quiet refuges where I not only was able to do my regular writing assignments, I was able to find the "alone time" to pursue other genres like poetry and short fiction, which I had dreamed about yet never truly pursued because I allowed fear and diversions to block my way.

It was daunting, at first, to pack and leave and start over again every few months in a new place with different levels of responsibility, new pets, and neighborhood, yet soon I viewed each experience like a blank page, something to fill up by exploring new terrains, or examining the inner terrain accompanied by my newfound solitude.

Sometimes it was scary. Other times it was exciting and fun. What I came away with is the conviction that I am my own gatekeeper, with the keys to open outward or inward. Although my house- and pet-sitting days are long over, I continue this transformation by relying on two elements: tea and meditation.

I began to approach meditation with curiosity, and, as Ram Dass wrote in *Fierce Grace*, "inviting your [my] fears over for tea." Tea had been a writing subject and a personal passion for years; however, meditation was new. In the beginning, on the advice and counsel of a friend, I began to sit quietly each day and "not think."

The first day I lasted about a minute.

The rattle-rattle in my head was deafening. The next day, I lasted a minute again. I could not let go of the fear that if I was still and let myself be at rest there would be nothing there. Or, there would be things I did not want to know or be reminded about. The fear was so intense, I abandoned the practice for weeks until my friend said, "Just try again." Imagine light or dark, he advised; invite good feelings, love, God, whatever you want, to pour into your being and go to that place of stillness that can quiet the mind completely.

*When we cannot bear to be alone, it means we do not properly value the only companion we will have from birth to death—ourselves.*

—Eda LeShan
(1922–2002)

THE NEXT MORNING, I sat upright on my chair, relaxed my arms, breathed in and out with a few deep breaths, and invited dark velvet to drape over me. I continued my measured breathing. I thought of the dark velvet under me, over me, behind me, in front of me. I do not know how long I was in that state when a thought interrupted, saying, "I feel so relaxed, like in a dream." I opened my eyes and noticed that I had been meditating for twenty minutes. Eureka! What was really exciting was how great and energized I felt, and the feeling lasted throughout the day. I believed that I had made a new beginning, a new start. The next day, I tried again, and, although I conjured up the thoughts in the same way, the experience only lasted ten minutes. Remembering my previous success, I knew I was finally getting to the point where this tentative step toward a meditation practice was becoming a natural, welcoming experience, and slowly, surely, continuously, over many weeks, I "got there."

This type of meditation practice, sitting and thinking of nothing, is a real challenge to anyone with a to-do list, much less a list to keep track of her lists. I explored many forms of meditation and share with you in this book the ones that really helped me to get onto and stay on the path of persistent practice.

That road was, and is, not always even. It is an evolving experience. Sometimes old habits cloud the rhythm: I oversleep and dash out the door for a plane or hurry through the morning ablutions to get to an appointment. I supplant physical meditation with morning dreaming. I do yoga instead. When I do not meditate, I miss it. I miss it with my body, with my mind, with my heart, and this feeling of loss is what encourages me to return to meditation as soon as I can; perhaps that evening, or the next morning.

ONE OF THE KEYS to getting the most out of any meditation is to surrender to the breath: measured, rhythmic breathing does more to de-stress than anything you can imagine. The breathing exercises explored in this book are adapted from many sources, following my studies with voice teachers, in classes for Pilates, yoga, Kabbalah, Buddhist meditation practice, and many other methods and philosophies that use breathing techniques to improve health, stamina, and well-being. They all work; breathing exercises require no equipment and can be done anywhere. Just as we cannot live without breathing in and out, learning to breathe deeper, more consciously, helps us to live more fully.

After that first successful meditation, I felt the need to acknowledge this accomplishment. With a renewed awareness of my senses and my surroundings, I chose a very special tea, and prepared it with even more attention and care than normally. I then selected a fine, beautifully handmade cup that I had been "saving" for a special occasion. Finally, I drank tea from this cup in honor of my meditation practice.

In the following chapters I have written down those meditation experiences that have been the most powerful or comforting to me, along with suggestions for two teas, one a premier tea for the tea connoisseur or the tea enthusiast looking for more adventurous flavors, and one "off the shelf" tea for those who are either totally new to this wonderful beverage or charmed by these more familiar, more accessible choices. (For a mini primer on tea, read "Tea: The Simplicity of Leaf and Water," on page 120.)

Tea has, for several thousand years and with good reason, been the singular beverage of those who meditate. Tea relaxes the body, stimulates the mind, and tastes delicious. Buy the best you can afford to drink following meditation; it is less expensive than a visit to a psychologist or physician, easier to swallow than pills, and has health benefits that are only now beginning to be documented. Medical studies demonstrate the healthful impact of regular tea drinking on preserving teeth and bones, nourishing nerves, decreasing fat levels, sustaining memory, and more.

Look around your house for those cups or teapots that mean something important to you. Select one or two that you will use only for this practice. (Or buy a new one, for nobody has enough teacups.) Choose a mat or pillow dedicated to your meditation practice, or a chair that allows you to sit up comfortably to breathe deeply, if that is easier. You are ready to begin! It might be a bumpy road at first, you may discover a detour—or many, as I did—but keep on traveling; I promise you, the destination is divine.

Come, let us begin the journey to meditations with tea . . .

*Meditations with Tea*

# Tea Meditations Defined

*Everything harmonizes with me, which is harmonious to thee, O Universe. Nothing for me is too early or too late, which is in due time for thee. Everything is fruit to me which thy seasons bring, O nature; from thee are all things, in thee are all things, to thee all things return.*

—Marcus Aurelius (121–180)

How did you awaken this morning? Did you bound out of bed, dash into the shower, grab a quick bite to eat, then head out the door? How will you retire tonight? Will you scribble out a to-do list, call the office, kiss the family members good-night, then plop into bed without ever stopping during the day to rest and reflect, even for ten minutes? Do you ever even remember falling asleep?

Probably nobody lives that frantically every day, yet as the world seems to speed up, so do we. Food can cook in minutes, sometimes even seconds. Travel to places it once took months to reach now can be done during a day or two. Instead of waiting a week for a letter or a newspaper to report an event, the news—with photographs—arrives almost immediately. For many of us, the telephone has been supplanted by email, enabling communication around the world or around town, without regard to time, availability of the receiver—or higher rates. Work, play, even thinking, is now done at heightened speeds, and there is so much to learn, to accomplish, to give, to relish. Today is a very exciting time to be alive . . . *and yet.*

Growing numbers of people, like you, are wondering if you could awaken slowly, with the sun; take time to prepare for the day; eat breakfast leisurely with family; and perform your daily tasks with purpose and less urgency. Then, at day's end, you could go to bed fulfilled, less worried, content, and certainly more aware of what the day was really like.

"Simplify!" is an edict of many artists and philosophers. Artist Hans Hoffman has said, "The ability to simplify means to eliminate the unnecessary so that the necessary may speak." Using meditations with tea can simplify your life.

Maybe you are already beginning the journey to mindful living, taking time to garden, even if it is only herbs in the kitchen or a window flower box. Perhaps you have regained the pleasure of music practice, or hand-writing personal letters, and treasuring the ones you receive. Possibly you are rediscovering the relaxation that comes from preparing a meal from scratch once a week or learning how to make something with your hands. If any of these activities is already a part of your life, you can well understand their benefits to be relaxing, restoring, and, yes, meditative.

For millions of people, for centuries, mindful preparation of tea and drinking it with intent has been a form of meditation that brings healthful results. It is easy to learn, powerful to do, and can be performed in any place where there is access to good water, tea, and a vessel to drink it from. Meditations with tea are, literally, fuel for body and mind.

*There is a fellowship more quiet even than solitude, and which, rightly understood, is solitude made perfect.*

—Robert Louis Stevenson (1850–1894)

> *It seemed to be a*
> *necessary ritual*
> *that he should*
> *prepare himself*
> *for sleep by*
> *meditating under*
> *the solemnity of*
> *the night sky . . .*
> *a mysterious*
> *transaction*
> *between the*
> *infinity of the*
> *soul and the*
> *infinity of the*
> *universe.*
>
> —Victor Hugo
> (1802–1885)

# Mini History of Meditations with Tea

## TEA AND MEDITATION IN CHINA

HOW DID THE ANCIENT idea of meditations with tea begin? The story of its origins harkens back several thousand years ago to China, most likely with Shên Nung, a sagelike emperor who was also an herbalist of great knowledge and gifted in writing down his discoveries for posterity.

One balmy spring day, so the fable goes, Shên Nung was relaxing following an invigorating walk to pick herbs and flowers for his research. He sat down under a large sweet-smelling tree to rest, and his servant started a small fire to heat water for brewing the herbs they had picked. A gentle wind blew their way and shook a few leaves from the tree under which the emperor was sitting. The leaves danced down through the air and into the boiling water. Concerned, the servant immediately attempted to scoop them out, when his master asked him to let the strange leaves remain in the water, for he was entranced by their aroma. The emperor asked the servant for a cup of the fragrant water and was pleasantly surprised by what he tasted. It was delicious; it made him feel calm yet alert. He sipped the liquid loveliness again, and, convinced that he had discovered something magical, he gathered up some of these new leaves to take back to the palace, and thereby made the first study of the evergreen Chinese camellia from which all true tea is derived, *Camellia sinensis.* (All other "tea" is properly called an herbal infusion because it is made from plants, flowers, herbs, or tree leaves or bark.)

Tea, like many plants, was first used as medicine. Its metamorphosis into the most popular beverage in the world, after water, is directly related to those monks from India to East Asia and points in between who readily recognized its unique combination of characteristics: It could relax the body while keeping the mind alert, two critical assets necessary for long periods of contemplation and meditation.

As the popularity of tea grew in China and moved on to Korea, Japan, and other points throughout Asia, monks began to not only drink tea, but also to save the seeds of the tea tree and carry them to each new destination, planting them, harvesting the leaves, then processing them into teas. The monks welcomed the delicacy in fragrance and taste of tea and its efficacy in keeping them alert during their hours of meditation. Soon, tea became, and has remained, the preferred beverage of monks throughout the world.

"THE SELF is Peace: that Self am I.
The Self is Strength; that Self am I."
What needs this trembling strife
With phantom threats of Form and Time and
Space?

Could once my Life
Be shorn of their illusion, and efface
From its clear heaven that stormful imagery,
My Self were seen
An Essence free, unchanging, strong, serene.

—Paul Hookham

## TEA AND MEDITATION IN INDIA

In India, there lived a handsome wealthy prince who believed that he needed to see the world and to achieve enlightenment. He gave up all the comfort of his station and left his home to travel on foot, seeking knowledge and then spreading his message. Along the way, he became a prominent figure among the legends of the origin of tea. One vivid tale begins with his frustration about falling asleep while attempting a prolonged period of meditation.

6

Angry with himself, he cut off his eyelids, threw them onto the ground, and right at that very spot, the first tea bushes began to sprout in India.

As dramatic as this is, it is largely apocryphal, for wild tea plants were known in northern India for generations. Bodhidharma, the name the prince took after his enlightenment, is considered the father of Ch'an (Zen) Buddhism by many. He was instrumental in carrying not only his message of enlightenment to the world, he also extolled the benefits of tea to his many followers.

During the nineteenth century, the British, after many attempts, finally were able to transplant Chinese cuttings of the tea bush into the hills of Darjeeling, thus creating a new industry and introducing billions more to the pleasure of tea. India is now among the largest producers of tea in the world. Today most scholars assert that *Camellia sinensis* originated in China and that the wild plant discovered in India is actually another variety, *Camellia assamica*.

Today, tea remains a conduit to meditation in the monastic world, and to all those who follow the many forms of meditation that have evolved. This very simple beverage elevates awareness and helps bring peace to all those willing to bring time and attention to its preparation and sincerity to its pleasures of fragrance and taste.

# What Meditations with Tea
# Can Do for You

*All beginnings require that you unlock new doors.*

—Rabbi Nachman of Bratslav (1772–1810)

THE MEDITATIONS in this book are guidelines only. They reflect my own interpretations of classic meditation practices and breathing exercises I have experienced. I hope they will inspire you, encourage you, help you in your quest for personal peace, and become a foundation from which you can develop your own meditation time with tea. Breathing and stretching exercises are listed with some meditations, and each practice includes two suggestions for teas to achieve either relaxation or stimulation. You can switch teas and meditation suggestions, leave some out, and think of others to enjoy as you explore both the meditation experience and the plethora of choices for teas available to you. This objective always is to bring your entire being to the meditation with tea practice and allow it to help you go where you want to go, or even to remain just where you are.

No matter how you use these suggestions, the single most important constant is the gift of quiet, uninterrupted time. And it is you who gives the gift to yourself: ten to twenty minutes as often as you desire it, in a place or places that contribute to the experience, like a corner alcove in your home or the lushness of a public garden, or simply shutting the door to the employees' lounge.

When you make time for yourself in a consistent way, family, friends, co-workers, and other people in your life will soon understand that this is *your* quiet time, and they will learn to respect it. If you take it seriously, others around you will take it seriously. Certainly, when the benefits of these meditations with tea are revealed, others will not only understand, they may soon follow in your path.

## REARRANGING PRIORITIES

### Buji kore kijin

*Doing nothing is respectable at tea.*

—Traditional Japanese saying

We each have twenty-four hours a day. How we "spend" those hours is directly related to what kind of day we have. We must eat, sleep, work, care for family, and, yes, we must care for ourselves. One of the most difficult ideas to get across to some people is that they are indeed in charge of their own lives.

Beginning today, remind yourself that *you can*.

*You can* say no to invitations.

*You can* say no to requests for time outside of work (and often at work).

*You can* say no to television, obsessive housecleaning, volunteer activities, and other requests for your time and attention.

Each day, you can honor yourself when you prioritize your tasks in order of importance, and you stick to the priorities. You owe it to yourself, and to others around you, to honor yourself in this way. Taking care of yourself should always be on top of the list because if you are not well mentally, spiritually, and physically, you cannot be of help to anyone else.

## What Would Be on Your Ideal Priority List?

You could list loving, laughing, hugging a friend, reaching out to a child, relishing your accomplishments, taking pride in your work, and taking pleasure in play. You could list playing sports and gardening and practicing an instrument, or singing a song or basking in the sun or viewing the sun rising and setting. Such simple pleasures these, you may say. Can you recall the last time you did any of them? Wouldn't today be a grand time for at least one of them?

As your guide to *Meditations with Tea*, I suggest noting, in red ink, the following item on your priority list: "Take ten minutes for a meditative cup of tea." Think you do not have the time? Rethink how you fill up the day and what tasks are really necessary, what you can put off to do another time, or delegate to someone else, or not do at all. Still feel there is not enough time for one more item on the "to-do" list? Be wild! Delete something from the list! Put off the dusting. Eliminate *something*. If you cannot, then ask yourself whether you are doing your absolute best by keeping so busy. Are you really accomplishing a lot by multitasking, or would you be more productive if you would focus completely on one task at a time?

Consider waking up twenty minutes earlier or staying up twenty minutes later and giving yourself this gift of tea and tranquility. You need it. You deserve it. You will benefit from it, because it will help you put the other things you do during the day in better perspective, allowing you the discretion to select which duties are really important.

Meditation is possible at any time in any place, with or without tea, but why not double this pleasure with a cup of your favorite tea? A client or repair technician calls to say that he'll be late? Use the delay to do a breathing exercise or daydream instead of raging against the interruption to your schedule. Think of ways to have goods and services delivered rather than running around town looking for parking places and using up your energy. It is worth any small stipend to have dry cleaning delivered, order supplies online, or even have the UPS pick up holiday packages to be sent on time.

## LEARN TO USE THE "D" WORD: DELEGATE

Share the load with the children, the spouse, the other family members. It will make them feel like important contributors to the household, and it will help to eliminate the feeling that all the burden is on your shoulders alone. You will still be loved, most likely will be appreciated more, and most important of all, you will be teaching the idea that your family is a unit that honors and supports one another.

Overwhelmed at work? Figure out how to delegate or share tasks with colleagues. Practice delegating, and it will become easier and easier. If something is too difficult or too onerous for you, ask if someone else would like to do it. You may be pleasantly surprised. To you, filing may be tedious, for others, it is a meditative experience! If it takes you more than eight hours to do your job each day, question each task you do for its importance, its relevance, its need to be done this very day.

Think about swapping duties. You may dislike phone calls, yet enjoy writing correspondence. See if someone will exchange these tasks with you. You may even carry this exchange idea as far as swapping jobs or sharing jobs where you each become a part-time worker, freeing you to pursue a graduate degree, spend time developing your own business, or spend more time with your family. You don't know until you ask. Reviewing what you do and how to make it ultimately satisfying can be very rewarding for both company and employees.

## MAKING ROOM FOR PERSONAL MEDITATION

*Since the garden path is*
*Beyond this transient world*
*Why not shake off the dust*
*Which soils the mind?*
—Sen no Rikyû (1522–1591)

Depending on where you live and with whom, finding a quiet corner and time may be a challenge. However, with intent, everything is possible. Look for objects of beauty to influence your experience: favorite artwork, objects you adore—even the beauty of the teacup or teapot you are using—flowers from the garden or the florist, a vista from your home or in your neighborhood, like trees, flowers, water, birds, anything that brings you a feeling of calm. It is ironic that for some people being alone in the car with a thermos of tea and no traffic, children, or weather reports to listen to is truly *the* meditative moment. If that is your idea of quiet time, do it. Park the car, push the seat back a few millimeters, sip your tea, rest, relax, ruminate—now you are meditating!

Your meditation alcove can be many places:

- Indoors in a supportive chair by the fireplace. Some libraries and bookstores have created wonderful nooks where you can curl up and read a book. Why not use one of them to have your quiet time?

- The bathroom may be the last sacred place for privacy. Hang a DO NOT DISTURB sign on the door, step into a warm bath, and relax, dream, take yourself away from the outside world.

- Your bedroom should be a balm; subdued colors, inviting bedclothes, quiet. Take advantage of it during the daytime to sit or lie down quietly to enter your meditative moment.

- Being among nature is magnificent, whether in a garden or the park, in a teepee or camping tent, while hiking, rock climbing, whatever outdoor activities you like. Stop a while to absorb the gorgeous scenery.

No matter where you work or go to school, there is always one place that is not being used. Scout out the building for an empty boardroom, a rooftop or outdoor area, the library, an empty classroom. Sit there for the quiet, the comfort of this temporary emptiness. Let the space and the absence of chatter restore you and give you strength for the rest of the day.

Traveling requires a keen awareness of time to make deadlines, take meetings, visit sites, even attend entertainment events. It is very important to give yourself the space for "alone time" to meditate when traveling. This will empower you in ways you might not realize. You will be sharper and more alert for business transactions, better able to relate to new people, places, and things you will encounter. Making time for meditation can actually make traveling exciting and fun again.

## Make an Appointment for Meditation for You!

Meditating on a regular basis will soon become second nature, just as natural as bathing, brushing your teeth, eating. For some, it may take some getting used to. I know, because I started and stopped many times. As a result, I came up with some suggestions that may work for you as they did for me.

First, why not make an appointment with yourself to get used to "quiet time"? Begin with drinking a cup of tea. Choose soft music over the din of the television, then choose silence over music to accompany your tea drinking. Let your mind wander during these first few times. No, do *not* bring your day-book or a to-do list to the table. All you need is you, your thoughts, memories, dreams for tomorrow, along with the warming pleasure of your tea.

Be realistic and do not attach yourself to specific outcomes. Try this for a limited amount of time, perhaps once a week. You will discover as most people do that you look forward to this meditation practice, and that eagerness will enable you to do it perhaps twice a week, then every other day, and then daily. Do not rush it. Release your anxiety about being "perfect" and just let the experience grow with you organically, naturally.

# Guidelines for Beginner's Breathing

*It is not necessary that you leave the house. Remain at your table and listen. Do not even listen, only wait. Do not even wait, be wholly still and alone. The world will present itself to you for its unmasking, it can do no other, in ecstasy it will writhe at your feet.*

—Franz Kafka (1883–1924)

*Quiet* is essential for a meditative moment. Some people have the ability to literally shut out noise around them, go into that deep center of consciousness, and rest. Others can focus on their work even in the midst of a storm. But for fruitful meditation, the stillness of "unnoise" is important. Select a place at home or away where you can be still, quiet, alone. You may be unused to silence, or uncomfortable with aloneness, believing it to be a relative of loneliness. It is not. Quiet is only beneficial. With it, you can hear the whoosh of the wind, the songs of birds, the rustle of leaves, sounds normally overwhelmed by traffic, chatter, the clutter and detritus of our noisy world. Welcome the silence.

*Being comfortable* welcomes the spirit of meditation. You can sit, lie down, or recline. Relax. Take off your shoes, loosen your belt, remove anything tight, from earrings to your watchband.

## Preparing for Breathing

FOR THESE BREATHING EXERCISES, choose a comfortable pillow on the floor, or a chair that supports your back so that you can breathe easily and deeply. Lying down on a sturdy mattress or couch is fine, too, but sitting while breathing is much better for you. Empty your mind as you would empty the trash can on your computer screen. Close your eyes and allow your body to absorb everything around you via your senses.

- What do you hear? Embrace the silence.
- What do you smell? Inhale the clean, fresh air and the perfume of flowers and grass nearby.

- How do the chair, bed, or cushions feel? Silky and soft to your touch, comfortable or firm, supportive?

- Can you empty your mind of busy scenes?

## DEEP-BREATHING EXERCISE

Now that you are sitting comfortably, and your sensory antennae are on alert, hold your head high and relax your shoulders. Sitting upright during breathing exercises is critical to improving lung capacity, and breathing in a way that is healthful and beneficial. This is an ideal meditation exercise to slip into your workday to re-energize you when you feel stressed or fatigued.

Allow your hands to fall by your side, or rest them in your lap, with the top of your right hand lying lightly in the palm of your left hand. Close your eyes. Breathe in as deeply and as slowly as you can and exhale deeply and slowly. Inhale and exhale four times. Sit quietly, breathing naturally and concentrating on the rhythm of your breath. Take note of how your head and neck and shoulders feel. Sense how your back and derriere and legs feel. They should feel totally connected to your breath. When you feel your body is completely relaxed, open your eyes, and sit for another minute.

## ALTERNATE NOSTRIL BREATHING

In alternate nostril breathing, you breathe in one nostril and exhale out of the other. To help you get started, gently place your right forefinger on your right nostril and inhale through the left nostril, using a count of four to slow down the inhale. Then, exhale from your left nostril for the count of four. The left nostril is particularly important as an aid to de-stressing and relaxing.

Next, place your left forefinger on your left nostril and inhale through your right nostril for the count of four, then exhale from your right nostril for the count of four. *Do not rush.* Try to inhale and exhale slowly, Repeat this alternative nostril style of breathing four times or until you feel a calm coming over you.

Remain sitting quietly. You are all the levels of your consciousness, awareness and subconscious, dream and nightmare, thought and memory. Continue to sit quietly. Accept what surfaces. Why? Has a doctor ever told you to finish a bottle of medicine even though you are feeling a lot better? The reason is that fragments of the illness may linger even if no symptoms are present, and they can cause problems in the future. That is the way it is with troubling thoughts; they will linger and cause bigger problems unless they are addressed, painful though this may be. So whenever anything surfaces that is troubling, or exciting or inspirational, listen. Write these things down. Then, close your eyes again and mentally tell your muse that you have heard the message.

When you feel completely relaxed, open your eyes and arise slowly. You will discover that all your senses are awakened, and what better time to enjoy your meditative cup of tea?

## Preparing Your Tea

YOU WILL NO DOUBT experience every action with increased clarity and purpose following a meditation or breathing exercise. In particular, note how your body feels as you prepare a cup of tea for yourself. The leaves, the cup, the kettle; everything should appear clearer, sharper. Scents should be more intense. You will be more able to brew your tea with patience, to give it the attention and concentration needed to do this simple act well. And you will be able to drink your carefully made tea slowly, with intent, savoring the fragrance, the color, the taste more fully than ever before. As you perform any or every one of the meditation or breathing suggestions in this book, take note of how they enhance the pleasure you get from the simple act of preparing and drinking tea.

When you are finished with your tea moment, rinse out your tea-making equipment and dry it before putting everything away in its special place. Leave your meditation alcove as orderly as it was when you approached it to begin today's meditations with tea. You will discover that your energy and awareness are thoroughly awakened as a result of your short vacation of quiet meditation with tea.

*While there's tea there's hope.*

—Sir Arthur Wing Pinero (1855–1934), British actor/playwright/essayist

## Tea: Breakfast Blends

If you have ever sipped a "breakfast tea," you probably had a blend of black teas from Kenya, China, Ceylon, and/or India. These blends are chosen for the balance among fragrance, color, and "body," which refers to how the tea tastes. A "full-bodied" taste is the ultimate for breakfast blends. Most of these are named "English Breakfast Tea" or its heartier relative, " Irish Breakfast Tea." These blends are available everywhere in a variety of styles and qualities. Loose leaf and tea bags, for iced tea or hot, black tea blends are the staples of the marketplace. Go beyond the familiar next time and try another brand, another type, something you have never tasted before. You may be pleasantly astonished. After all, the world of tea offers thousands of choices to savor.

*Thank God for tea! What would the world do without tea?—how did it exist? I am glad I was not born before tea.*

—Rev. Sydney Smith (1771–1845), English clergyman and writer

## Tea: Assam

For an unblended choice, try an Assam (*Camellia assamica*). These large-leaf teas from the northern Indian state of Assam are indigenous to that country (before the smaller Chinese varieties were successfully imported for planting). Assams are smooth and rich and hearty, and excellent with or without milk. Breakfast teas are so named because they are a lively full-caffeine burst of beverage to have in the morning. If caffeine is a concern, you can decaffeinate the tea yourself, and be assured that no chemical decaffeination was used. See the directions on the next page.

# How to Decaffeinate Tea at Home

Bring water to nearly boiling and pour on the tea. Let it infuse thirty seconds in the cup and discard the liquid. Pour hot water on the leaves again, and infuse in the cup for two minutes or longer to taste. Because nearly 96 to 98 percent of the caffeine is infused out of the leaves during the first cup, your second infusion will be practically caffeine-free. Enjoy. ❧

# Brewing Basics Review, or How to Make Tea That Tastes Great

Each of the meditations in this book is matched with two suggestions for tea that include a premium tea and a familiar commercial choice. With the easy accessibility of online and mail-order sources, good quality tea is readily available, and you owe yourself the pleasure of drinking it. Most tea vendors offer sample packs that are modestly priced ways to explore a variety of teas. Be adventurous!

The choices for teas are growing each year, thanks to creative packagers, imaginative "noses" who create recipes for tea blends, and better and easier access to smaller single-estate tea farms and the increased enthusiasm for organically grown teas. In particular, green tea has become enormously popular for its health benefits. Green tea is not made like your typical English Breakfast tea. It requires water temperature that is much lower, and steeping time that is much shorter (see page 25 for details).

When experiencing new teas, it is always a good idea to ask your tea vendor for his/her advice about quantity, temperature, and brewing time. Although all true teas come from the same botanical plant, they are not all processed the same way, and require slight to substantial changes in brewing to elicit the full flavor. The result of such minor homework is major satisfaction in the cup.

To get the most out of any tea, drink it plain, without milk, sugar, lemon, or other flavorings. Some black teas, such as Indian Assams or Chinese Keemuns, take well to milk. Always sample them plain first to see how you like them that way: Milk does alter the flavor and may not be necessary.

When buying loose leaf teas, take some in your hand, crush the leaves, and sniff. The tea should have a fresh, pleasant fragrance. You are looking for the same qualities that you would in good produce: good color and fragrance in the dried leaf, which should lead to good color and fragrance in the infused leaf, and, the final arbiter, good taste in the mouth.

## Quantity

Fine quality teas require fewer leaves to produce good flavor in the cup. However, the lighter and bigger the leaves, the greater the quantity needed to make that flavorful cup. When in doubt, use about a teaspoon of tea to each four ounces of water. Adjust to taste. Subsequent infusions often make stronger brews, although some teas weaken after several infusions. Here again, ask your vendor for suggestions on how many infusions each tea should make, and how they should taste.

## Water

Water is as important to the preparation of tea as the tea leaves. If your city has fine tap water, please use that; however the finest choice is spring water. Some excellent brands, both foreign and domestic, are Poland Spring, Volvic, Music, and Calistoga. Taste the water by itself first; if it doesn't please you plain it will not make satisfactory cups of tea. Some spring waters have so little mineral content that they make a flat-tasting cup of tea. Tea leaves require some minerals to interact with to bring out full complexity of flavor.

Tap water filtered by a commercial filtering system attached to the water source is an alternate water choice and is usually better than packaged purified waters. Distilled waters are best used for irons and curling rods; they don't contain the natural minerals to interact with the tea leaves. Although some tea vendors believe this is a good quality, most do not. As always, let your palate be your guide, for it is the only one you need to satisfy.

## Temperature and Time

Temperature and steeping times are also critical to a great cup of tea, and time is more important than temperature. Strangely, some Chinese greens require up to seven minutes to elicit the best flavor, even though most greens require barely thirty seconds of steeping, and some blacks taste better at one to three minutes per serving even though most blenders recommend five to seven minutes.

When in doubt, it is always better to err on the side of underbrewing, for you can always continued to brew—whereas overbrewing makes tea so undrinkable that even diluting it with additional water will not save it.

Whenever you buy a new tea, ask the tea vendor his/her suggestions for water temperature and brewing time. If you buy a packaged tea, follow the recommendation of the company, then adjust according to your taste. You can use a small timer if brewing tea away from view of the kitchen clock.

Below are some suggested times for brewing high-quality teas. You will note that boiling water is *not* used. Fine teas release their nectar better in water that is slightly cooler than boiling. If you do boil the water, allow it to cool a minute or two, or simply put a tablespoon of cold water in the pot to cool the temperature. It is that simple. With experience, you will soon know when the kettle has reached the proper temperature.

If you like a scientific approach, use a candy thermometer and put it into the kettle or saucepan when you first see small bubbles appear, when the bubbles get larger, and when they are roiling. A roiling boil is not necessary, no matter what has been said or written before; it simply expels too much oxygen from the water and makes tea taste flat. Use spring or purified water unless your municipal water is superb. Again, do not use distilled water.

## GUIDE

**Whites** should barely be steeped, about thirty seconds in 175–185° F water

**Greens** should be steeped thirty to forty-five seconds in 185–190° F water

Whites and greens can be steeped longer on subsequent infusions (high-quality whites and greens will offer at least two quality infusions, and often more).

**Oolongs** should be steeped one to three minutes in 190° F water

**Blacks** can be steeped two to five minutes in 195–200° F water

*Note: All of these times and temperatures are suggestions;* always ask your tea vendor for recommendations for brewing temperatures and times. Teas, even those from the same estate, change from season to season, year to year, and may need more or less brewing time than before, so the savvy tea drinker chooses a tea vendor wisely and follows his or her advice. If your tea vendor cannot answer these questions, he/she may not be cupping (tasting) the teas as new ones are delivered. If this is true, find another vendor! Tea is ephemeral, elusive, concrete, subtle, pronounced, a little of everything. That is part of the essence of adventures with tea. 🍃

MEDITATION 2

*Elevating Energy*

*Love silence, even in the mind; for thoughts are
to that, as words to the body. . . . True silence is the
rest of the mind, and is to the spirit what sleep is
to the body, nourishment and refreshment. . . . It is
a great virtue.*

—William Penn (1644–1718)

## JUST-SIT STRETCH

This meditative exercise will empower you to do more, think clearly, and feel stronger. And it is the perfect prelude to an afternoon tea break.

Sit up in a chair with the entire back of your thighs on the seat. This position helps you sit up straighter without strain. Allow your arms to drop to your sides, then hunch up your shoulders as close to your ears as possible, hold to the count of four, then slowly lower your shoulders back to their normal position. Repeat.

## FLYING BIRD STRETCH

Next, hold out your arms as if you were a bird flying. Stretch your arms outward as far as you can, so that you feel the muscles of your hands, forearms, and upper arms being pulled. Hold that position for the count of four, then relax your arms, and drop them against your sides. Repeat.

Hold out your arms again; this time hold your hands palms down and imagine that you are pushing them down through water. Push, push, push, and very slowly let your arms rest at your sides. Begin again, but this time, lift your hands, palms up, from your sides, and imagine that you are lifting through water. Lift, lift, lift very slowly until your arms are parallel to your shoulders, then slowly lower them back to your sides, keeping your palms up.

## Peek-a-Boo/Lookie-Loo Stretch

Finally, sit comfortably, arms at your sides or with your hands resting lightly in your lap. Slowly and carefully stretch your neck upward as if you are trying to see over the top of a barrier. Hold that position for the count of four, then slowly lower your neck and relax. Repeat.

> *Your vision will become clear only when you look into your heart. Who looks outside, dreams. Who looks inside, awakens.*
>
> —Carl Gustav Jung (1875–1961)

## Lovely Leg Stretch

While sitting in a chair, lift your left leg parallel to the floor, and stretch it as far as you can, holding for the count of four, then lower your leg so that your foot touches the floor. Lift your right leg parallel to the floor, and stretch it as far as you can, holding it outward for the count of four, then lower your leg slowly until your foot touches the floor. Repeat.

How do you feel? Calm? Alert? Energized?

*Inhale the sweet smell emanating from the tea as the hot water liberates its essence. Feel a growing sense of relaxation as the mind focus is drawn to the rhythmic movements of breath. Inhale the vital energy life force. Exhale the energy of union with the universe. Allow yourself to fall gently into deep concentration on the space just following the exhale. Deeper and deeper the universe expands, moving through translucent space that shimmers like a black pearl. In this moment, tea is brought to your lips by a slow steady hand. A taste bitter sweet as life itself.*

—James Burnett (b. 1949), environmentalist, president of The Ecology Works®

## Tea: Orange Spice

Now you are ready to complete this Energy Meditation by drinking a cup of tea, one that will enhance the energizing experience of your meditation. Orange or other citrus, known for its energizing qualities, is a good choice for an afternoon pick-me-up. Try an orange spice or lemon tea. If commercially prepared flavored teas leave something to be desired, you can always blend in some fresh lemon or orange zest to your dried tea leaves before infusing, to get the same extra boost of citrus in the cup. Orange is a vibrant color that suggests happiness and liveliness. Consider using an orange cup or mug, orange napkins, or placemat for your pleasure.

> *Louisa was slow and still in her movements; it took her a long time to prepare her tea; but when ready it was set forth with as much grace as if she had been a veritable guest to her own self. The little square table stood exactly in the centre of the kitchen, and was covered with a starched linen cloth whose border pattern of flowers glistened. Louisa had a damask napkin on her tea-tray, where were arranged a cut-glass tumbler full of teaspoons, a silver cream-pitcher, a china sugar-bowl, and one pink china cup and saucer.*
>
> —Mary E. Wilkins Freeman (1852–1930)

# Tea: Darjeeling, the "Champagne of Teas"

Darjeeling is always a welcomed, refreshing tea. Its apricot fragrance and orange-red color in the cup will enhance the experience of drinking it nearly as much as will its ambrosial taste. Darjeeling blends are legion, so seek out premier single-estate teas like a Makaibari, or Selimbong for a true champagne taste of tea.

Choose a small teapot, pour hot water into it, and cover with the lid. This will warm the pot in readiness for the tea. Heat the water to almost boiling, then allow it to cool for about a minute or longer. Pour out the hot water from the teapot, put a teaspoon of tea into the warmed pot, then pour the heated water over the leaves and allow to brew for one minute. Taste for strength, and brew longer, in one-minute increments, until it is to your taste. Pour the tea through a sieve into your cup or mug. It is always best to pour out all the liquid when using a teapot. If the water is left inside the pot, it will continue to steep, actually stew, and the subsequent cups of tea will be bitter. If possible, drink your tea outside for a fresh-air break, or at least drink it away from where you regularly work, because a change of view can be as refreshing as a cup of tea.

# "Just" Walking

Long conversations
Beside blooming irises
Joys of life on the road

—Matsuo Bashō (1644–1694)

## WALKING AFTER BUDDHIST
## SITTING MEDITATION

In the community of Zen Buddhist monks, a walking meditation (*kinhin*) is done as an extension of the meditation done sitting (*zazen*) to give the body a way to be refreshed, yet keep the mind in its meditative state. One "just" sits or "just" walks, to be totally connected with the task at hand, be it sitting, sweeping the ground, cooking, or, yes, walking.

Legend has it that the Buddha himself performed walking meditation, done slowly, mindfully, and in his day, in the forest following a sitting meditation in front of a tree or in a wooden hut.

Getting the most out of a walking meditation requires that you turn on your sensory antennae just as you do when sitting or lying down to meditate. In this way, you can become keenly aware of your feet touching the floor or ground, aware of your posture and your breathing, and aware of the earth and trees and sky around you without actually turning your head or body to observe them.

This method of walking works best when you match step with breath. For example, to walk in step with your breath, slow down your regular walking pace. Next, inhale and exhale, then take a step; inhale and exhale, then take another step. Inhale and exhale. Repeat until you develop a rhythm of breathing then walking, breathing then walking, and this rhythm will soon become natural to you.

Where you walk is as important as how you walk. This is not a stroll or a hike, but a form of meditation while walking. So to avoid unnecessary distractions, you can walk in your meditation room inside your home, or go outside and walk a well-worn path, go back and forth through your backyard, patio, driveway, or even around an empty garage. Walk in a straight line, moving the right foot first, then the left. When you turn, turn to the right.

You can hold your hands in the same way you do while sitting. Some of the ways to position your hands include:

- Rest one hand in the palm of another horizontally, with your thumbs touching.
- Rest your hands upon your thighs, holding your thumb and forefinger together.
- Hold your left hand in a loose fist in your open right hand.
- Use your right hand to cover the loose fist of your left hand.

Choose whichever position feels comfortable. Connecting your hands together rather than keeping them by your side will help keep the focus of your meditative experience alive and the energy flowing within you.

While walking, maintain, as much as possible, the inhale/exhale/step pace, and walk for five to ten minutes or longer, as desired. When you feel that your legs are rested and relaxed, return to where you were sitting and continue your meditation, or choose this time to end your meditation and prepare for your tea.

*When tea is made with water drawn from*
*the depths of mind*
*Whose bottom is beyond measure,*
*We really have what is called chanoyu.*

—Shogun Toyotomi Hideyoshi (1536–1598)

## TEA: GYOKURO

The "Precious Dew" green tea of Japan, Gyokuro would be a fitting beverage for the conclusion of this meditation. The elegant, long, hunter-green leaves are deeply fragrant, and brew up an exquisite pale green liquor. Pour into white or clear cups to get the most visual pleasure from this tea. The leaves will give you several small cups of exquisite drinking. Take care to brew with slightly under-boiling water, and taste after thirty seconds. Brew longer to taste. The flavor should be like drinking liquid sweet-grass sugar.

## WALKING THE LABYRINTH

The labyrinth is a form of walking meditation whose over 4,000 years of history has evolved into a twenty-first-century tool for de-stressing and prayer. Prehistoric rock

*Breath is*
*the bridge which*
*connects life to*
*consciousness,*
*which unites your*
*body to your*
*thoughts.*
*Whenever your*
*mind becomes*
*scattered, use your*
*breath as the*
*means to take*
*hold of your*
*consciousness.*

—Thich Nhat
Hanh (Thây)
(b. 1926)

carvings have been found in Spain and Italy reflecting the existence of labyrinths in those countries, some early Greek coins depict labyrinths, and during medieval times, the mystical Kabbalah teachings of Judaism and the Christian Church both used forms of labyrinths as spiritual tools. They have been found in Sweden, in Native American culture, and throughout Europe; the most famous one still in use was installed in Chartres Cathedral, near Paris, in 1201.

One might hardly believe that "walking around in circles" could be meditative, but its singular style of repetition and the focus and attention required to follow the outlined path become another way to go outside of oneself and find a state of peace. Both private and public labyrinths are currently being constructed throughout the country, some following the classic designs of the Chartres labyrinth and others from antiquity, and some contemporary ones with interpretations that reflect the personality of the owner. Some are literally inside churches with the markings painted or built up upon the floor, others are outside, creating a formalized pathway among the lushness of nature. Newer ones—some plain and others gloriously complex—can be found in hospitals, schools, parks, and retreats. You can enter a labyrinth during daylight, or experience them under the light of the moon or strategically placed lamps.

From above, a labyrinth looks like a series of broken circles, like a maze, yet it has only one entrance and no dead ends, so it is not confusing or difficult to walk it. One simply starts at the beginning and walks through the open pathways with a steady, pensive pace. The objective is to allow the body to move while the mind empties of stress and thought and fears and doubts. After walking a labyrinth, people often remark that they come away refreshed, able to see clearly solutions to problems they have tried to figure out, or, as the ancient Roman adage revealed, *Solvitur ambulando*, the solution comes through walking.

Technically, what happens when people walk a labyrinth is that our "left brain," the one that speaks in logic and reality, is continuously occupied by following the narrow constrictions of the pathway around the labyrinth. You cannot get lost, really, and yet you can lose yourself at the same time. That signals our "right brain," that center for intuition, creativity, and imagination, to become released, set free.

Although one could sit at different points along a labyrinth, do yoga, dance, kneel to pray, the most beneficial way to incorporate its power into your consciousness is to walk it. Whenever you feel frustrated or in despair, walking meditation, walking a labyrinth, or "just" walking can free your mind to think and give you a genuine feeling of peace. Following the walk, you may find it helpful to write down your thoughts or talk them over with friends over a cup of tea. To enhance the reassuring feeling of the walk, opt for a calming tea that is beautiful to see when infused, like a peony.

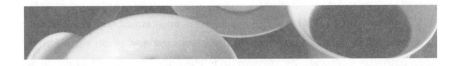

*Drink your tea slowly and reverently,*
*As if it is the axis on which the whole earth revolves—*
*Slowly, evenly, without rushing toward the future.*
*Live the actual moment.*
*Only this moment is life.*

—Thich Nhat Hanh (Thây)

## Tea: Peony

An example of "mudans," a category of shapes formed with Chinese tea leaves, the peony is a wonderful tea for entertaining. Mudans are made by tying tea leaves together or weaving them in such a way that they form a shape for which they are named: peony, anemone, strawberry, rosette, hummingbird's nest, and numerous others. They are an ideal choice of tea to take along with you and a thermos of hot water because they can be infused for up to thirty minutes. Simply put the mudan in a cup and cover with water. Take your walk, then return to drink its delicate brew. You will be greeted with both a light-tasting tea and the visual surprise of seeing your peony "bloom" into shape because it has been infused. Mudans are usually made from either green or black teas. Brewing them in a clear glass cup, wineglass, or similar vessel adds to the fun.

# MEDITATION 4

## Asking Forgiveness

*As I rejected amnesty, so I reject revenge. I ask all Americans who ever asked for goodness and mercy in their lives, who ever sought forgiveness for their trespasses, to join in rehabilitating all the casualties of the tragic conflict of the past.*

—President Gerald R. Ford (b. 1913)

*W*e human beings are capable of such grace . . . and such cruelty. From standing someone up for a date to leaving someone standing at the altar, from hurling racial or religious epithets to dropping bombs, we do the unforgivable. World leaders sometimes abandon principles for power over others and employers sometimes abandon considerate management over profit at any cost. Employees sometimes embezzle, steal, cheat. We are all vulnerable to temptation, and who has not ever practiced some deception or distraction from the truth?

It may help to remember that many of those who are cruel do not care how we view their deeds; they are not wondering how to apologize; they may even feel their behavior is "right." In forgiving others, we can do something to ease our personal pain. It is not only possible to forgive, it may even be critically imperative for our own well-being. Yet forgiveness takes time and effort. Amends must be made. Justice must be sought. Apologies, true and authentic, are a beginning. How do we bring ourselves back to a point of grace? How do we forgive others and move beyond the painful memories?

> *I speak in grief,*
> *No exultation, for I hate no more,*
> *As then ere misery made me wise.*
>
> —Aeschylus

If there is a legal avenue to pursue toward a just conclusion, by all means pursue it. If there is a way to sit down and discuss your feelings with those who have hurt you, consider doing that, with or without professional counselors or arbitrators. If there is only the blank page or canvas on which to express your feelings, fill it up edge to edge. If you can literally move away from those who have hurt you, do it; a change of venue can be a healthful first step to healing. Your opponents will continue to "win" if you continue to view them as such.

Do not believe you are alone or have to face your dilemma alone. Seek help from therapists, your spiritual leaders, your true friends, and people, places, and things that bring you comfort. Being a victim is not a point of honor; remaining a victim keeps the victor in power. Take that away from him or her. Throw off the albatross of victimization and move beyond. Then, and only then, will you be able to fill your heart with forgiveness.

Childhood bullies terrorize others because they do not know any other way to get attention. They feel jealousy, loss, less. By embracing a bully, inviting him to play, a child can turn a bully into a friend. Author-illustrator Maurice Sendak, commenting on the revival of the concentration camp play *Brundibar* in the June 2, 2003, issue of *Time* magazine, said, "I wanted to handle my situation creatively [his childhood memories of learning about the Holocaust]. . . ." Sendak believes there is something positive about turning "bad or evil feelings into something you can live with and explore and even exploit."

Thinking creatively about the hurts and traumas of childhood may not be so simple for a child to do, but when he is engaged by the tools of quiet time to think and consider all the possibilities, assisted by loving attention from his parents or mentors, it is truly amazing what positive things a child can imagine as a way to work out the situation.

*Never be afraid to sit and think a while.*

—Lorraine Hansberry (1930–1965)

It is nearly impossible to change an adult bully, because he may not have benefited from the intervention of true friendship or love, and he can be expected to continue his lifelong method of taking instead of sharing, hurting instead of loving, even though he aches with longing for connection. If he has family, he can pass on his behavior to his children and begin a cruel legacy that traps his descendants. One way to reach such a "bully" is to treat him only with kindness, with compassion, with love. By offering kindness instead of fear, we may be able to allay his bad behavior. At the very least, we can confuse him long enough to devise "plan B" or seek help to diffuse the situation.

*Come listen, O Love, to the voice of the dove,*
*Come, hearken and hear him say,*
*There are many To-morrows, my Love, my Love,—*
*There is only one To-day.*

—Joaquin Miller (1837–1913)

# Meditations on Forgiveness

*Since nothing
we intend is ever
faultless, and
nothing we attempt
ever without error,
and nothing we
achieve without
some measure of
finitude and
fallibility we call
humanness, we
are saved by
forgiveness.*

—David Augsburger,
American
theologian

THIS PRELUDE TO THE ACT of forgiveness incorporates tangible things that can help set you free from anger, mistrust, or unrelenting grief. Choose artifacts that are symbolic of what or who you would like to forgive. They could be photographs, mementos, or books. It is so personal an act that only you can decide what these items should be.

One way to participate in this process is to write a letter that outlines what happened and why you now believe you are ready to forgive. Read it out loud. Change the words as necessary, then place the letter among any mementos you have gathered. Consider lighting a candle and using its flame to imagine the hate and anger burning away. Similarly, you can place the letter in a flame-proof bowl and set it afire. As it burns to ashes, close your eyes, and repeat a mantra of your own choosing or say, "I forgive _____ for the pain caused to me, and I move on." Repeat five times or more, until you believe every word. Open your eyes.

Clear off the display. Make a decision right now about which artifacts to keep or give away. Do this today. Take the ashes and use them to feed compost, mulch a plant, or just bury them in the ground, knowing that what was once a declaration of pain and anger has now been converted into ash, something that can actually nourish a plant. As the plant grows and blossoms, may you find comfort in knowing that something that once ate away at you is now feeding life again and that you were able to make that transition happen through the act of forgiveness.

## Forgiving the Self

HOW DO WE FORGIVE ourselves for less-than-noble behavior toward others? Sometimes we feel guilty because we have said or done something for which we cannot forgive ourselves. If you feel that way, ask yourself if you can make amends. What can you do to apologize, repay, redo, to fill the void that your acts or words caused? Here, too, one can call, meet in person, write a letter, to begin the process. Then you need to ask that person to forgive you for the pain or loss you caused. You may discover that your apology is readily accepted, or you may need to face serious accountability.

Whatever it takes, it will be less than the pain of not forgiving yourself. If the person involved is now deceased, you can visit his/her grave, write a letter, pray or meditate on that person's being. Take action to repair and move on. Meditate on this passage and repeat: "I forgive myself

*Nowhere can man find a quieter or more untroubled retreat than in his own soul.*

—Marcus Aurelius (121–180)

45

for the pain I caused to ____. I ask forgiveness of myself for my acts and request the strength to move on." Repeat five times or more until you believe every word you say.

> *It has been well said that tea is suggestive of a thousand wants, from which spring the decencies and luxuries of civilization.*
>
> —Agnes Repplier (1858–1950)

## Tea: Formosa Oolong

Such a powerful act as forgiveness requires some affirmation, and nothing is as life-affirming as the joy of friendship. Invite someone you know to be funny and happy to join you for this important day. A perfect choice for tea is a Formosa (Taiwan) oolong, known for its beautiful floral scent redolent of springtime, the season of renewal. Oolongs are available in wide variety, and Formosa oolong can be found almost anywhere. Brew it according to the directions, or start with a heaping teaspoon of leaves, four ounces of hot water, and brew lightly, perhaps a minute or two, then taste. Brew longer as desired. The fragrance and the delicacy of the taste will be just the right accompaniments to time with your friend and will surely help you both savor the moments together.

# Tea: Silver Needle

If you prefer to drink your tea solo following this powerful forgiveness exercise, opt for a white tea, perhaps a Silver Needle dancing in a glass tumbler or in a beautiful white cup. It will provide you a delicate tea, easy on the stomach, and gentle on your body. To brew, place a teaspoon of tea in the tumbler and add about four ounces of hot water, heated up to (or cooled down to) about 185° F. The leaves will dance in the water, offering you a fascinating ballet to enjoy. You can drink the tea as is, or strain the leaves into another glass or cup.

# Offering Gratitude

*If the only prayer you say in your whole life is "thank you," that would suffice.*

—Meister Eckhart (1260–1328)

T eaching me how to say "please" and "thank you" was one of the first lessons my mother taught me when I was a little girl. As I grew, the lesson was expanded to expressing thanks for presents in a hand-written note, learning other rules of etiquette, and polishing the lessons until they became as natural as breathing. I am forever grateful to my mother for this, because as an adult I recognize that being aware and experienced with good manners gives me the confidence to be in any situation with anybody at any time.

Saying "please" and "thank you" is also part of spiritual practice, and nothing seems as important as expressing gratitude when health is recovered, fortune smiles, love walks in, or grief is abated. Counting blessings is a mantra in and of itself, and everyone has many, if we only look for them.

Creating a meditation for gratitude is a highly personal act that can be couched in the prayers of our faith or made entirely personal using our own words, songs, or poetry. Whether gratitude is expressed to a god or a friend or even a stranger who has helped us, the only hallmark that is necessary is sincerity, words from the heart.

## Writing Your Blessings Meditation

This meditation exercise begins with pen and paper. List everybody and everything for which you feel grateful. Take your time making the list. Compile it over an evening or over several days. You will soon realize the list has no end. Jot down additions to the list whenever you feel thankful; you will be astonished at how long your list of blessings will grow.

What is on your list so far? Health; love for your family, mate, friends and their love for you; clean sheets and a warm bed to sleep in; good food to eat and the skill to make it (or appreciate it); nature and all its wonders; the imagination of inventors and scientists who develop the ideas and things that make our lives easier; Western and Eastern medicine and its practitioners; satisfying work; invigorating sports; the ability to laugh (or be funny), love of learning. What else?

Ever have days when you're blue? When you feel down for reasons known or unknown? When you are scared or worried? That is exactly the time to take out this list and look it over. You will soon remember how your blessings are greater than your sorrows.

## GRATITUDE BREATHING EXERCISE

This is an exercise that is helpful for public speakers, singers, and anyone who needs to tap into the full potential of the lungs to gain power in the voice, whether offering song or thanks.

Sit up with your spine straight and the back of your thighs on the chair. Hold your hands, fingers up and palm-to-palm, together in front of your chest.

Purse your lips as if you are sipping a soda, and breathe in slowly and steadily and make the following motions with your arms: Release your palms and hold your hands out to either side of your body, then raise them gently over your head and put the palms together again while over your head, straightening your arms. Then release the breath slowly as you bring your arms in front of you, palms still together. Just as your palms are reaching your chest again, and you may believe you have no more breath to expel, stick your arms out straight in front of you, with palms still together, then release them and allow them to hang by your hips. Stretching out your arms in front of you will help strengthen your diaphragm. The exercise also enables your body to expand and contract the rib cage, as if it were an accordion, and will eventually build up your lung capacity.

Doing this exercise often is a way to build upper body strength while at the same time teaching your body to relax and breathe more deeply and naturally.

*The best state of mind in which to drink tea is one of deep meditation. The second best is while looking at a beautiful landscape or listening to music. The third best is during a stimulating conversation. In all cases it is necessary to aspire toward a quiet and tranquil frame of mind.*

—Attributed to Chinese Ch'an (Zen) Master Paichanng (749–814)

# Tea: Earl Grey

One of the most popular tea blends in the world, Earl Grey was first created as a gift to a prominent British gentleman named the Earl of Grey, who had provided discreet political services for a high-level mandarin in China. The mandarin was so grateful, he asked his tea masters to create a tea in honor of the earl. The finest black teas were blended with a rare and exotic fruit, a pear-shaped citrus known as bergamot, and a classic was born. Today, one can find many varieties of this blend. Experiment with a few until you discover one just right to express your gratitude. Brew a teaspoon of tea leaves to five ounces of water for three minutes, then taste. Brew longer as desired.

*Meanwhile, let us have a sip of tea. The afternoon glow is brightening the bamboos, the fountains are bubbling with delight, the soughing of the pines is heard in our kettle. Let us dream of evanescence, and linger in the beautiful foolishness of things.*

—Kakuzo Okakura (1862–1913)

# Tea: Pi Lo Chun

For the taste seekers among you, consider Pi Lo Chun, a tea with an "astounding fragrance," which also happens to be the English definition of its ancient name. Today, you can find it translated as Silver Spiral Green, Spiral Green Jade, Green Snail Spring, and similar names that reflect the small, twisted, curved leaves. It has a slightly sweet taste with a lingering delicate aftertaste that is the definite flavor profile of China varieties. Taiwanese (Formosa) varieties are even more fragrant but do not usually have twisted or curved leaves. Brew a heaping teaspoon of leaves in four ounces of hot water for one minute, or longer to taste.

# MEDITATION 6

## Shoring Up Creativity

*Visions come to prepared spirits.*

—Friedrich Kekule (1829–1896)

*C*reativity is a way of approaching anything you do with fresh eyes, a relaxed mind, and pure curiosity. Creativity is hardly the sole province of artists or writers. Who has not seen a totally dull piece of jewelry, or a boring movie? On the other hand, we have all been amused, surprised, excited about new features added to old appliances; new products, from Post-its to single-sheet aluminum foil packs; or new ideas that make the everyday errand simpler, like banking via the Internet or communicating via cellphone. It is the creative person who looks at problems and comes up with a solution, or looks at existing products or services and develops a new or easier way to work with them.

What interests you? What work do you do? How can you approach your job differently? What would make the end-user/customer benefit from your product or service? Ask customers what you can do to make business easier or products better. Do they suggest that you need to reduce waiting time or improve ordering procedures? Use your very own power of creativity to make it happen.

> *Let yourself be silently drawn by the stronger pull*
> *of what you really love.*
> —Mowlana Jalal al-Din Rumi (1207–1273)

From vocation to avocation, from leisure time to home responsibilities, you can make every aspect of your life stimulating, exciting, and satisfying with a touch of imagination. Your creative juices are always fermenting, let them "rise!"

But, wait, how do you get to these questions in the first place? How do you change the way you view your world and the people in it? How can you change how you behave or think or use your store of creativity?

One technique I have used for years is the twenty-minute "purposeful nap meditation." I think about a problem or a question, ask my subconscious to bring me an answer, then I literally sleep on it. I have become so adept at this that I sleep for twenty minutes exactly, and although most of my prized napping is just for renewed energy, I always come up with *some* answer to my question.

Think of a question that is as specific as possible to your situation. It could be "How can I negotiate a longer escrow for the clients who need more time to move?" or "Why do the wheels keep cracking on the kiddie truck we've designed?" or "What can I do to help get Suzie interested in math?" As you can see, the questions are not philosophical or abstract; they are specific to a need or desire. Write down questions to reflect any types of concerns or problems you may have. Use these questions in typical brainstorming sessions with colleagues or family. If you cannot get a satisfactory answer, then sleep on it with the "purposeful nap meditation."

## NAPPING MEDITATION

Sit on your bed and remove your shoes, then remove anything restrictive like a belt, or tight jewelry or a tie. Choose your own method of relaxing before napping or begin to slow down your breathing, and breathe in and out deeply through your nose.

Before lying down, you can ask your subconscious a question or consider a problem that needs solving. Think about the question you posed. Say it to yourself a few times. Breathe slowly and deeply, then lie down, get comfy, cover yourself up, sink into your favorite sleeping position, and rest.

Tell yourself you need to nap for twenty minutes. When you awaken, honor what surfaces. Take advantage of what the muses have to offer. It could be as revelatory as the cure for cancer or as mundane as how to get a babysitter for the kids Saturday night. The depth of the problem is not as important as meeting the urgency of the need.

You may not be able to actually sleep if you are not an experienced napper. This is not important, for just resting, just lying still and being calm is restorative. If you do fall asleep, great. And, like any other habit, practice makes it easier and easier.

## CIRCLE OF BREATH EXERCISE

All living things need oxygen: plants, trees, animals, and, of course, people. We can go without food for some time, we can do without water for a while, but none of us can last very long without breathing. When we stop breathing, we die. This breathing exercise has been used in birthing rooms for women in labor, in therapy sessions to initiate a feeling of rebirth, and in numerous applications to center people to relieve anxiety and distress.

It works particularly well when done while lying down . . . naptime or nighttime. Close your eyes and exhale deeply, imagining the breath going through your lungs and "out" your navel; then, breathing in deeply, the breath will follow a circle pattern from your navel back through your nose and down to your lungs. Repeat this "circle of breath" three times. If you do it deeply, you may experience some light-headedness, which has the interesting phenomenon of amping up all your senses so that you will see, hear, taste, smell, and feel on a deeper level.

Other creative applications to problem solving and solutions to the conundra of life require thinking in opposites. Instead of up, look down, in/out, backward/forward, past/present, outside the house/away from the company, whatever it takes to give you a fresh place to think through the questions you have.

## RECALL THE DREAM

Is a relationship stagnant or a marriage on the skids? Remember how it once was. What made it great? What were your goals then? Did you meet any of them? What could you do today to bring that social or working relationship back again? Is it time to move on?

## TAKE A BREAK

Do you want to ditch the job, bop the boss, evaporate the constantly interrupting colleagues? Before you do, take a vacation! Go somewhere you have never gone before, take scuba lessons or learn bookbinding, take a hike or revisit a favorite nature spot or hang out at home and read a book from that teetering stack piled next to the bed.

*Nothing can come out of nothing, any more than a thing can go back to nothing.*

—Marcus Aurelius

## Change the Routine

Drive a different route to the same destination. If you are the cook, make breakfast for dinner and lunch for breakfast. Delegate one daily task to someone else, or exchange one-on-one. Switch hairdressers or barbers, try a new restaurant, sleep naked if you like jammies or wear a nightshirt if you like to sleep in the buff. Call someone out of the blue to chat. *Try a new tea!*

*Everyone has talent. What is rare is the courage to follow the talent to the dark place where it leads.*

—Erica Jong (b. 1942)

## Kids Need a Break, Too

Invite your children to be parents and you be the kids for one day (age six and up is reasonable). Make a date with each person in your family and do what he or she wants to do. Wake everybody up earlier to watch the sunrise or keep them up late at night to see a predicted meteor shower. Instead of giving gifts, write your children a letter describing everything you adore about them. Read it to them at bedtime, no matter how old they are.

*A delicious pleasure overtook me . . . filling me with a precious essence: or, rather, this essence was not in me,*

*it was me . . .*

—Marcel Proust (1871–1922)

# Tea: Jasmine

The Persian flower jasmine found its way to China during the early years of the tenth century. Its addition to Chinese green teas makes for a heady, nearly intoxicating brew. Jasmine tea is often shaped into small round balls the size of 6 mm pearls, having beautiful elegant leaves in its highest grade, Yin Hao, and in other exquisite examples. The infusion provides a multisensory experience first by its scent, which echoes the exotically beautiful night-blooming flower; then by its taste, silky and smooth on the tongue, exquisite in its delicate flavor as it passes down your throat. Brew this with a light touch, and expect a liquid of pale, pale green best viewed in a stark white cup.

*Tea should be taken in solitude.*

—C. S. Lewis (1898–1962)

# Tea: Dragonwell (Lung Ching)

This China green can be a whole prism of flavors, reflecting the quality range of seven (or sometimes more) traditional grades. Dragonwell's signature flat, long dusty green leaves are elegant and full of flavor. They are grown throughout the province of Zhejiang, where there really is a Dragon's Well. Legend has it that a distraught monk prayed fervently for rain to save his crop of tea and the benevolent Chinese mythological dragon, symbol of water, provided all that was needed. Grateful to the dragon for his nourishing rain, the monk named this tea in his honor. Today it is called Lung Ching, Dragon's Well, and the fabled well still exists. This is a perfect tea to introduce yourself to the greens of China, with their signature nutty-sweet, non-astringent, lovely full mouth feel. Brew from thirty to forty-five seconds at first, taste, then brew longer as desired.

MEDITATION 7

# Being with Family

*Better is a dry morsel with quiet than a house full*

*of feasting with strife.*

—Proverbs 17:1

E very night at six o'clock, my family and I ate dinner together. Even
though my father kept his music store open from 9 A.M. to 9 P.M., he
always took time out to have dinner with us. We ate in a huge
kitchen with windows on two sides with a view of trees and plants, and
enjoyed homemade meals prepared by my mother. My parents would talk

about interesting things that happened in the store, or share stories about family; my sister and I talked about school or play or whatever intrigued us. We learned table manners and how to converse, some of this taught with intent, other things learned by osmosis. Afterward, not always willingly, my sister and I would help clear the table, wash and dry the dishes, then complete our homework, or read favorite books or watch television, still a relatively new invention then. It was an idyllic time, one for which I am grateful because it laid the foundation for me to cherish dinner time with family and friends.

> *There should be the greatest care imaginable, what impressions are given to children; that method which earliest awakens their understandings to love, duty, sobriety, just and honourable things, is to be preferred. Education is the stamp parents give their children; they pass for that they breed them, or less value perhaps, all their days. The world is in nothing more wanting and reprovable, both in precept and example; they do with their children as with their souls.*
>
> —William Penn

The term "family" can be defined in so many ways, not just involving the proverbial mother, father, and two children. The varieties of "family unit" are legion; the only criteria, really, is the presence of emotional support and care for one another, and the joy that comes from being with one another for the everyday and for the special occasion. Whatever form your family takes, consider enhancing or developing a ritual of "just being" with one another. Call it hanging out, spending the day, dropping by. If you do it with a rhythm of regularity, such as every Tuesday or the first Sunday of each month, or whatever fits your mutual schedules, you will find all of you looking forward to time spent together and you will feel like a family, a community, as in those who *commune*.

Leaving time for a spiritual coda is a life-affirming gesture, be it time spent attending a church service, prayers at home, reading religious texts, or simply holding hands with one another as you greet the Sabbath or acknowledge your blessings. The following two Iyengar yoga poses are intended to be done sitting, involve very little output of energy or time, yet are remarkably effective in achieving the desired result: connecting to the spirit in you and outside of you.

## SITTING POSE

This is a pose that should be done while sitting on a couple of folded blankets, a bolster, or firm pillow. Sit upright so that your breath can be deep and steady, and place your ankles on the opposite thighs in the classic cross-legged yoga position. If you're not that limber, sit with one ankle under the other, knees as close to the floor as you are able. Breathe normally but deeply, keeping your eyes open and "soft," which means neither gazing nor intently looking. Retain this position for thirty to sixty seconds. Gently unfold your legs, stretch them out in front of you, and slowly rise. For a powerful connection between family members, do this pose while holding hands with one another.

## QUIET TIME POSE

This exercise will remind some of you that your grade-school teacher really knew what she was doing when she asked you to lean over your desk and put your head down on your arms for a time out. It is a wonderful way to help the smallest children in the family enter the silence of meditation very simply, and a lovely prebedtime ritual to help quiet energetic little bodies and active minds. It is also a good relaxing technique for adults, anytime they need a few moments for their own time away from the duties of the day.

Sit on the edge of a chair and lean over a table or desk so that your chest and head can be supported by your arms on the tabletop. Breathe steadily, naturally, yet as deeply as you can. Retain this position for one to two minutes. Gently lift your head and chest upright, breathe in deeply again, and stand up slowly. Following this brief meditation, consider extending the moment with a dip into poetry.

For children, especially, a quiet time before sleeping is critical for the rest they need to build strong bodies. No ritual is as inviting or more cherished than bedtime reading, from *Mother Goose* to *Goodnight Moon*, from *A Child's Garden of Verses* to Dr. Seuss. Poetry, in particular, offers not only an entrée into the rhythms of speech, but also the music of language upon which children can dream, and conjure stories of their own. Read a poem as meditation today, with children, with a mate, or alone. Let the music of words bring you peace.

> *Such songs have power to quiet*
> *The restless pulse of care,*
> *And come like the benediction*
> *That follows after prayer.*
>
> *Then read from the treasured volume*
> *The poem of thy choice,*
> *And lend to the rhyme of the poet*
> *The beauty of thy voice.*
>
> *And the night shall be filled with music,*
> *And the cares, that infest the day,*
> *Shall fold their tents, like the Arabs,*
> *And as silently steal away.*

—Henry Wadsworth Longfellow (1807–1882)

*Savor the pleasure of chai, and your day will open like the petals of a flower.*

—East Indian saying

# Tea: Masala Chai

This is a great tea for the whole family. It is milky, sweet, spicy, and can be served as a hot and soothing beverage in the winter and as a refreshing iced drink in the summer. This recipe yields four small servings, and can be doubled or quadrupled as desired.

2 cups water

4 heaping tablespoons (or four teabags) black Nilgiri or Assam tea or breakfast blend

4 whole cloves

4 whole green cardamom pods

$1/2$ teaspoon freshly ground black pepper

1 large stick cinnamon

Dash fresh-grated ground nutmeg

2 slices fresh gingerroot

2 cups whole milk (or soy milk or condensed milk)

Hot water for warming cups

Sugar to taste

1. Boil the water, toss in tea and spices, and lower the heat to a simmer.

2. Brew for about five minutes, then pour in the milk slowly, and continue to simmer for two minutes longer.

3. Pour hot water into four small cups, then empty the cups of the hot water.

4. Strain tea and spices through a sieve into the now-heated cups. Sweeten to taste. (Sugar may also be added while masala chai mixture is simmering.) Simmering times are approximate; cook to your taste.

You will certainly realize that there are as many recipes for chai as there are chai lovers, and this recipe is just a beginning. Experiment with those flavors and spices you like most, be they allspice, star anise, various peppers from white to pink to black, cinnamon from China or Sri Lanka, black or green cardamom, seeds like fennel or coriander, or dried mace or nutmeg. Sugars are also full of possibilities: raw Hawaiian or turbinado, Indian chunk sugars, Demerara, crystals, and good old granulated white or brown. Some chai lovers enjoy using honey or molasses instead of sugar in their chai.

*Tea is the beverage of ceremonious people, and like the dense monsoon rains, it is both calming and stimulating, encouraging conversation and relaxation. . . . Ideas and traditions steep slowly in its steamy transparence.*

—Pascal Bruckner (b. 1948),
contemporary French novelist and author of *Parais*

# Tea: Sangria

Sangria is a Spanish wine cooler flooded with fresh fruit. Tea sangria is a nonalcoholic version that is equally as colorful and a perfect summer refreshment. Brew your favorite black tea, such as an Indian Nilgiri or a Ceylon orange pekoe, and set aside. Put in a pitcher, thinly sliced fresh fruit such as oranges, kiwi, strawberries or peaches. Arrange them in a decorative way; pack them in or layer them like a lasagna of fruit. Pour chilled tea over the fruit and serve. For ice, use cubes made of orange juice or tea so as not to dilute the Tea Sangria with more water.

Another version of fruited tea calls for black tea seasoned with dried fruit instead of fresh. You could use mango, pear, peaches, strawberries, or passionfruit. The tea's silky texture and aromatic perfume of fruit is naturally relaxing, and it tastes like summer even in the depths of December. The marketplace is jammed with packaged fruited teas, so the choices are many. If you are an enthusiastic cook, you'll love thinking up ideas for combining your favorite black teas with dried fruits for a "third" flavor.

MEDITATION 8

# Remembering the Sabbath

*Thus the heavens and the earth, and all the host of them, were finished. And on the seventh day God ended His work which He had done, and He rested on the seventh day from all His work which He had done. Then God blessed the seventh day and sanctified it, because in it He rested from all His work which God had created and made.*

*—Genesis 2:1–3*

*E*ven though different religions honor the Sabbath day differently (Muslims acknowledge the end of the week on Friday, Seventh-Day Adventists honor the Sabbath on Friday, Jews on Saturday, Christians on Sunday), choosing to remember the concept of the Sabbath is the focal point in this discussion. So, why not select your own Sabbath day if that is what you desire? Too much to do? Remember, if God can rest, so can you.

I have a friend who has made Thursday her Sabbath day simply because she works the other six days; another calls Wednesday his "Sacred Day" even though he attends Mass on Sunday. He uses the day to read, relax, and write in his journal. Another friend chose Monday instead of her regular Saturday to make it personal for herself. Monday in her community is a day when many places of distraction (shops, restaurants, theaters) are closed so she uses this as incentive to devote the day to one of true rest.

The Hebrew word *Shabbat* means "be still," "cease," or "rest." The Sabbath day is traditionally observed to remember what God has done and to remember His purpose for us through rest from work of all kinds. Sanctifying the spirit of God touches us through prayer and acknowledges the work He has done.

*Where there is no peace, prayers are not heard.*

—Rabbi Nachman
of Bratslav

71

## Rest to Refresh Meditations

On your Sabbath day, *rest*. True, you can simply stay at home or incorporate art or music or nature or other enriching experiences into your life, but above all make it an easy, simple day. It is amazing how going to the beach, strolling in an art museum, or penciling in an evening at the symphony can result in way too much activity for a Sabbath day. Even hanging out on the veranda with friends, or using the time to garden, sew, or do woodwork is the antithesis of the meaning of the Sabbath, the day of *rest*. *Slow down*.

Perhaps this is the time to re-read familiar religious texts or new ones: the Old Testament or the New, the Quran (Koran) or related works of philosophers, priests and rabbis, scholars, essayists, and hymnists. You could attend the quiet communal meeting of the Quakers who sit in silence, speak with a soft voice, or sing in a soft tone if the spirit so moves them. Read poetry. Recite it to one another. Take naps. Turn the answering machine on low and (this is hard, I know) do not check it or your email the whole day long. Order food in or eat leftovers. Cuddle your pets and nuzzle your loved ones. Talk to one another about ideas and dreams and things silly or serious. Move about *leisurely*.

*All that God asks you most pressingly is to go out*
*of yourself—and let God be God in you.*

—Meister Eckhart

If the "rest" is too difficult a goal right now, consider the mandate to "Sing unto Him a joyful noise." The raucous tremor of full-out gospel singing can carry believers into a different state. The whirling dervishes use their twirling dances to enter a dizzying altered state of consciousness that they believe brings them closer to their Maker. The shaking standing prayers of the eponymous "Shakers" was a physical expression of their love for their god just as much as how native peoples everywhere use drums and dance and song to carry their messages upward to their Great Father and bring themselves into a state of peace.

Music can also be a gentle consolation, a pathway to dreams, inner contemplation, relief from the cacophony of mindless chatter or chaotic news commentary. Music, particularly instrumental music, can help relax the body, quiet the nerves, calm the heart. And, there is a unique silence associated with it, in pauses or "rests" between notes or phrases, and in the quiet expectation just before music begins and the stillness of satisfaction when it ends. Both these times of silence are special because of the quality and beauty of the music heard in between. Music can help "soothe the beast" in our minds and our hearts, and help us make a worthy transition from activity to restful prayer.

Whether quiet or filled with "joyful noise," our prayers are surely meditative, for they lift us outside of our busy minds and anxious bodies and into a place of tranquility. However you choose to worship or pray is up to you, for it is *for* you. And however you choose to honor your Sabbath day, consider the long-term benefits of rest. "And God saw what He had done, and was pleased, and He rested."

*Let the words of my mouth, and the meditation of my heart,*
*be acceptable in thy sight, O Lord, my strength,*
*and my redeemer.*

—Psalm 19:14

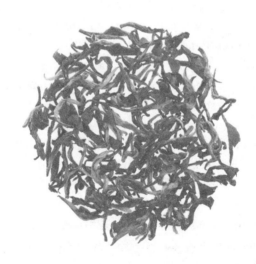

*You can taste and feel, but not describe, the exquisite state*
*of repose produced by tea, that precious drink, which drives*
*away the five causes of sorrow.*

—Chinese Emperor Ch'ien Lung (1710–1789)

# Tea: Ti Kwan Yin
# (Iron Goddess of Mercy)

An oolong tea named for a goddess of legend, Kwan Yin, Ti Kwan Yin is as fabled a beverage as the story behind it. One day, many many years ago, Kwan Yin tested the faith of a young Chinese man who prayed to her for a solution to the spiraling descent into poverty that his community was enduring. Upon hearing his prayer, the marble white statue of Kwan Yin came alive and stretched out her long elegant arm to a scraggly plant on the edge of the gazebo that housed her. "See that plant," she said. "It is my gift to you. Nurture it, water it, and soon it will provide what your village needs." The young man was awed and perplexed, but for weeks, he pruned the plant, watered it, and saw that it was growing under his care. As it emerged from its former scraggly, weedy appearance, the young man realized what it was, the *Camellia sinensis*, the tea bush. Excited, he shared the news with his fellow villagers, and they soon were planting the seeds of this plant all over the village and harvesting its leaves for the beverage now known as cha, or tea. They named their famous tea after the goddess of mercy, Kwan Yin, and its rich, dark, aromatic brew has been like a blessing to all who love tea. Today, Ti Kwan Yin (Iron Goddess of Mercy) is available in great quantity and is the perfect tea to begin or end a Sabbath day.

> *This morning's tea*
> *Makes yesterday*
> *Distant.*
> —Japanese Tankô poem

## Tea: Genmaicha

A Japanese green tea with plenty of personality—you might even say it has snap, crackle, and pop—*genmaicha* is blended with roasted rice kernel hulls and popped corn to provide a light roasty green flavor. It is wonderful for an afternoon break, a delicious tea to share with family members of all ages, and goes very well with most foods. Brew lightly, two minutes or less, to best release the nutty-roasty fragrance and taste. Some varieties include sprinkles of *matcha*, the powdered green tea for the Japanese tea ceremony. This makes an intriguing sharp contrast with the sweet aftertaste of typical *genmaicha*.

# MEDITATION 9

## Doing Business Mindfully

*The most important habit is solitude, quiet time. People who enter their day by taking forty-five minutes or an hour for themselves—meditation, prayer, inspirational reading, taking a walk—before they go for it in the real world do their best.*

—Ken Blanchard (b. 1940)

*B*ringing the concept of meditation into the workplace may seem like an oxymoronic concept to high-energy, Type A business people, but there is growing evidence that taking time out to rest is as important during the working hours as it is at the end of your day.

Most workers have the benefit of a mandated coffee break of fifteen minutes in the morning and fifteen minutes in the afternoon. However, instead of taking a break, too many people run errands (in person or on the phone), answer email, play on the computer, or worse, work through the break. Even though the demands of the day sometimes require ignoring regularly scheduled breaks, that does not always mean better productivity.

Because increasing production is at the heart of all business, doesn't it make sense to incorporate meditation practice in the workplace? Whether you are management, staff, a small business owner, or on the assembly line, consider meditating at least ten minutes of your work day, at least one day a week. Hesitant? Here are a few ways of using meditation to do business mindfully in your work environment:

- Come to work fifteen minutes earlier and use that time to prepare for the day by meditating privately. If you have an office or an employees lounge, close the door, shut your eyes for a few minutes, and do a breathing or resting meditation. It's healthier than a sweet roll, and longer lasting, too.

- When the weather is good, go outside and do a breathing and walking meditation. Nothing clears the head quicker than fresh air, a change of scenery, and a few minutes of mindful meditation. And, when the weather is bad, do a walking meditation down hallways or around your desk.

✎ At the next staff or board meeting, share how meditation has made you more productive or creative. Suggest that prior to any problem-solving or brainstorming sessions that each person meditate in their own way; share your favorite techniques, or better yet, ask that a spiritual practitioner come to the next meeting to demonstrate meditation techniques for business-centered people. Your management will be surprised how much imagination surfaces from a few minutes of meditation, especially with expert guidance.

✎ Just as solo meditation practice is further enjoyed with a cup of tea, an enjoyable tea experience can elevate any meeting into an "event," so include fine tea in any meeting or brainstorming session you attend. Or why not suggest that the firm provide high-quality tea and equipment in the break room or employee lounge, so that all employees and your fellow colleagues can enjoy this experience on their own? When management places a priority on employee well-being—even if it's by offering something as simple and as inexpensive as quality tea—the effort will certainly elevate morale. What an economical and easy-to-achieve effort to aid production!

*A man is not idle because he is absorbed in thought.*
*There is visible labor and there is invisible labor.*

—Victor Hugo (1802–1885)

The custom of serving tea prior to or as a conclusion to a business meeting is practically universal. Even those countries that have a coffee culture—Italy, Brazil or Spain, for example—are seeing a birth of tea bars and tea rooms.

How can you present tea in your business meetings? You have studied your clients' business, you have made efforts to learn the proper protocol to conduct business with international clients, and now it is time to make your objectives happen.

The easiest way to begin is to meet in a luxuriously-appointed five-star hotel lobby or private concierge level where you can be assured that tea service will be discreet, elegant, and readily accepted by most. For those people whose culture or religion forbids true teas, herbal infusions can be served.

An unexpected but thoughtful way to begin or conclude business with your international guests at your headquarters is to serve them tea in their style, which may mean a fine hobnail pot and excellent gyokuro tea for Japanese customers, English style tea service for European business associates, or using beautiful gung fu sets or gaiwans to serve Chinese clients.

It is not, however, the style of tea service that is important; it is the quality of the tea and the precision of the service. Provide the highest-quality tea you can find, brewed and served graciously, yet inconspicuously.

If you decide to offer tea in a style that reflects the culture of your client, seek out a shop in your area, and arrange for an experienced tea server to come to your meeting place. Hiring someone to do this may be the best investment in customer relations you'll ever make.

The most important reason to serve tea mindfully to clients is that all of you will be noticeably relaxed and comforted by the tea. At the same time, it will make everyone alert and aware of the business objectives on the agenda.

Nothing demonstrates respect for your clients more than offering them handmade cups, special teas, heirloom teapots, or accoutrements. This simple, personal token will seal the effort you have made to acknowledge, understand, and demonstrate respect for a significant part of their culture.

*You have to have your heart in the business and the business*
*in your heart.*

—Thomas J. Watson, Jr. (1914–1993)

*In the taste of a single cup of tea you will eventually discover*
*the truth of all the ten thousand forms in the universe.*

—Attributed to the Venerable Kyongbong Sunim,
Ch'an (Zen) Master

# Tea: Yunnan Black or Green

A province in China, Yunnan is famous for its steady production of a rich, smooth tea that is processed either as a black or as a green. The black is lightly floral in fragrance, which belies its deep flavor, a full-mouth feel, and great satisfaction. It is perfect as an afternoon tea, or to conclude a meal. The green Yunnan is quite a bit heartier than other Chinese greens, and is an interesting tea to introduce to someone new to green teas. Brew a teaspoon of leaves to five ounces of underboiling water for one minute, taste, then brew longer as desired.

> *Tea does our fancy aid,*
> *Repress those vapours which the head invade*
> *And keeps that palace of the soul serene.*
> —Edmund Waller (1606–1687)

# Tea: Mao Feng

When I first was introduced to this richly aromatic and evocative green tea at a formal tasting, I made a fool of myself. I kept going back and back for more. I bought a half-pound, a huge amount for me, took it home, and drank it all up, savoring the intense fragrance and lingering sweetness with each and every cup. Now I purchase Mao Feng in considerably smaller quantities and use it for special occasions—which amazingly come up for little or no reason. This is my idea of a tribute tea, a beneficiary of the mist and clouds of the mountaintops in Anhui province, harvested after the first rains. It is a totally Chinese tea, still quite rare, dearly expensive, and remarkably satisfying. I cannot think of a better tea to close a deal, sign a contract, end a convention of like minds. Brew in a *guywan* then pour into a ceramic pitcher. Use the pitcher to pour the tea into a thimble cup or small handleless cup. Steeping time varies; begin with one minute and brew longer to your taste.

# MEDITATION 10

## Caring for Community

*The deepest feeling always shows itself in silence.*

—Marianne Moore (1887–1972)

In Mainland China, the words of greeting translate to "Have you had tea?" reflecting how natural and all encompassing is tea drinking in that vast country of many cultures and customs. Drinking tea is convivial, a way to say hello to friends and family, casual, elegant, a way of life. You can find a merchant drinking tea from an old glass jar with silver needle green tea leaves dancing through the infusion. She will fill the jar with water several times a day to reinfuse her tea.

Or grandpa will sit among the chirping of finches in bamboo cages at the local teahouse, smoking, telling tales taller than he, and using a covered cup, a *guywan*, to paddle the large leaves through the water to infuse his tea. Even in his old age, the man can balance the *guywan* gracefully, holding the saucer firmly in his hand, bringing the cup to his lips, and sipping through the opening made by the lid dipped slightly into the infusion. The *guywan* can also be used as a vessel from which a host can pour the tea into small cups.

Some rural farmers grow and process tea for their own use from small patches of bushes, others need to buy tea from local sources. Tea is so plentiful; it is always fresh, usually green, sometimes *pu-erh* or oolong. Black tea, called "red tea" for its reddish hue in the cup, was the first effort at product stabilization for the growing European market that still buys it in awesome quantities. The unprocessed white and green tea, however, is what most Chinese drink each day.

At home, friends and family gather around the dining table to enjoy a steaming pot of tea poured into handle-less cups, warming their hands before sipping the tea, knowing that a cup that is too hot to touch contains tea that is too hot to drink. Everyone will talk about the day, the gossip of community, with ever-wary eyes on the children. It's a family even if the group is not related: old and young, middle-aged and infants, drinking tea and talking all at once in one communal breath. Is this a form of meditation? I say yes, because while sitting among friends and family, sharing stories and tea, we lose self-involving thoughts and pay heed to the joy of being with one another. When everyone rises from the table and the tea things are put away, we are left with a mellowness and softness that is the blessing of drinking tea with those we care about.

# Taiwanese Preparation
## as Meditation

### GUNG FU, OR THE ART OF DOING THINGS WELL

IN TAIWAN (Formosa), an island just east of Mainland China, the complicated and fascinating category of oolong tea reigns supreme. You can choose from lightly oxidized *pouchongs*, still green in color in the leaf and in the cup, or various gradations of color and intensity of flavor up to the darkest oolongs, sweet, floral-rich in fragrance, and pure poetry in a cup.

One popular custom of tea service is the *gung fu* ceremony, an intriguing combination of ritual and hospitality. The tea accessories are sometimes set upon a drainer, a round flat container with a lid that has holes in it. This very clever item is a way to pour water or spent tea into the container without the need to leave the table. Afterward, it can be emptied and cleaned easily and swiftly. If a drainer is unavailable, a wide, flat bowl may be used to cradle the pot and the cup. Water and tea waste can be poured into that bowl and discarded later. A neatly folded hand cloth is at the ready to catch drips or to wipe up any spills that may occur.

A caddy holds bamboo or wooden utensils that include a tea scoop; tongs for handling the small cups; and a teapot needle that has a blunt end on one side and a pointed end on the other. The pointed end is to dislodge infused leaves that may get stuck in the spout of the teapot and the blunt end is used to clear out leaves from the body of the pot. These utensils help the host or hostess prepare tea without ever having hands touching the delicate tea leaves. As an extra precaution, perfumes and scented or waxy lotions should be avoided when making tea.

The pot and cups for this ceremony look nearly doll-like because they are so small: the little teapot accommodates the large-leaf oolong teas and just a small amount of hot water, thus providing an intensely flavored tea liquor. The small size of the pot allows the host to completely decant the tea with each serving and to reinfuse the leaves with hot water several times, thus preventing the bitterness that can occur when the tea leaves are left in to continue steeping.

Two cups are part of this ritual: a fragrance cup and a drinking cup. The fragrance cup is cylindrical and narrow, about three inches high and one inch across. The host first pours the tea into this cup, which is then passed around the table for each guest to be stimulated by the wonderful fragrance. Then the guests may pour the tea from the fragrance cup into the tasting cup or the host will pour tea from the pot into the cup. The teacups are lined up and the host pours the tea in a horizontal line backward and forward until all the cups are filled. By pouring the tea in this manner rather than pouring each teacup individually to the top, the hosts insure that each guest receives the same taste and temperature of tea. As noted above, a *guywan* can be substituted for a small teapot as the vessel from which tea is poured into the little cups.

Ah, the *gung fu* cups! They are tiny, a little wider than an inch across and barely an inch high, and accommodate at most a tablespoon of tea. These "thimble cups" help to slow down and stretch out the tea-drinking experience. Rather than drinking the tea, one sips it, savoring the many flavor profiles experienced in the front and back of the mouth, all the while absorbing the intoxicating fragrance.

The ritual begins when the guests are seated. The host proceeds to pour hot water onto the cups, and with the tongs, to empty them. This helps to heat the cups and serves to wash away any dust or other foreign matter. The host then pours hot water into the pot and empties it for the same reason. Tea is scooped out of its caddy and placed in the pot, and hot water is poured over the tea, but then discarded. In this way, any dust or fannings from the tea are washed away, the leaves are "awakened," and the tea is ready to be infused.

Finally, hot water is poured over the leaves, allowed to steep the proper time, and then the tea is served. Special caution is made to place the forefinger on the lid and to firmly grasp the pot's handle with the other fingers so that pouring is gracefully and neatly done. Each guest may pick up a cup; or the host may hand it to the guest, using his forefinger and thumb; or the host may place the cup upon a small matching saucer (or little tray) and set it before each guest. The tea is reinfused and the drinking continues in a congenial, relaxed atmosphere and, as desired, sweet or spicy snacks or Chinese-style *dim sum* may be served, but are not necessary.

# The Four Principles of Chanoyu

Most "Japanese tea ceremonies" in the United States reflect the Urasenke School which began during the sixteenth century. Two other schools, less well known, offer different styles of presentation: they are Mushanokôjisenke and Omotesenke.

The sixteenth-century tea master Sen no Rikyû is credited with ritualizing and formalizing *chado*, the "way of tea." Combining the rigid discipline of his warrior and regal sponsors with a sensitivity to art and beauty, Rikyû developed a ceremony that embodied philosophy as much as it celebrated the pleasures of tea. The four philosophical principles are harmony, respect, purity, and tranquility, that, he believed, should be integrated in the sharing of tea and in daily life to demonstrate pureness of spirit. These principles are represented by four "acts" of the ceremony, in which one act segues into another so that at the end, both ritual and aesthetics are seamlessly blended.

**Harmony (Wa)** crystallizes the sharing of tea between host and guest, an interaction emphasizing the idea that *chanoyu* is not a solitary pursuit. The feeling of harmony in a well-balanced garden is as important as the harmony of the interior of the tearoom, where the tangibles of tea service are balanced with the harmony of the guests— the result being a sense of peace.

**Respect (Kei)** The concept of respect permeates the entire *chanoyu* experience, from host to guests, from guests to host, and also from all to the very utensils handled in the ceremony. They are regarded to be valuable, whether they are newly made and modest or heirloom bowls as much as a hundred years old.

**Purity (Sei)** Washing the dust from the world begins in the gardens and along the pathway toward the teahouse. Both are swept of detritus and meticulously prepared for the visiting guests. At the doorway, guests pour water over their hands to symbolically cleanse themselves before stepping through the short door, lowered to imply that all who enter are of equal stature. All who enter The Way (of Tea) are attired in clean and neat clothing without extravagance and come to the experience with a pureness of heart and spirit.

**Tranquility (Jaku)** The highly trained tea master is the embodiment of tranquility, derived from years of practice in the way of tea, a way of life that meshes *chanoyu*'s ideals of harmony, respect, and purity. His selfless grace and hospitality become a natural extension of his tea art and are the ultimate gift from tea host to gracious and respectful guests. The Way, the tea masters teach, provides "endless possibility" in the lives of both host and guests.

# Japanese Tea Preparation
## as Meditation

### CHANOYU—HOT WATER FOR TEA

DISCRETION, RESERVE, elegance, and the beautiful thread of heirloom art of the tea bowl make up the ritual of *chanoyu*. The way of tea is one of equanimity, where all guests are equal regardless of station in life, and where the severe serenity of the simple tea hut is an inducement to pay heed to the teahouse and the people in it. The Japanese have a phrase, *chazen ichimi*, or "Zen and tea are one," which thoroughly captures the heritage of *chanoyu*, which began with Chinese monks bringing the message of Zen to Japan, and along with them, the seeds for the tea plant.

Acknowledging beauty and art is part of the contribution of the guests to the host, perhaps admiring the single scroll of a poem written with exquisite calligraphy or the single seasonal blossom that peeks out over an equally stunning vase created by an esteemed potter.

The meditative aspects are many but most vibrantly, all of the senses are engaged, the view of the trees and plants in the gardens, the fragrance of the tea, the tatami, the incense in the tea house, the rustle of the wind among the trees, the soft echo of footsteps approaching the doorway of the hut, and, finally, the sound of the water heating over the brazier. The sensitivity of touch is part of the meditative approach to handling and admiring the tea bowl and examining the utensils when passed to the guests. Finally, taste is engaged when the tea is savored along with any sweet, snacks, or small meal that is served. Surely the stimulation of all one's senses underscores the value of tea as "spiritual medicine."

The *chanoyu* can be a one- to four-hour ritual with many choreographed steps in the greeting of guests, admiration of the teahouse and the utensils, preparation of the fire, and preparation and serving of the tea, snacks, and the conversation among the guests. The intense concentration of the host to prepare the tea mindfully and beautifully and the respect offered in turn by the guests, has a remarkably relaxing effect. One cannot think of worldly cares in the teahouse; one is in another, more peaceful world, where a combination of meditation and tea are artfully joined.

*A Buddhist master was asked by one of his students how he could put the enlightenment of meditation into action. "By eating and by sleeping," he replied. The student exclaimed the obvious, "But everybody sleeps and everybody eats." The master answered, "Not everybody eats when they eat. Not everybody sleeps when they sleep. This is the wisdom of ordinariness, that all action be done with intent," the Master added.*

## Sencha-do

During the eighteenth century, the venerable tea seller Baisa-o helped to popularize another type of tea ceremony, *sencha-do*, the way of *sencha*, the everyday green tea of Japan. Baisa-o was instrumental in championing the artists of the day, *bunjin*, who sought *en*, a feeling of freedom and equality to pursue their literary and painterly arts although living under a demanding feudal system of government. Serving and drinking tea was important to these calligraphers and artists, poets and fiction writers, historians and scholars. Much less formal than *chanoyu*, *sencha-do* did much to cultivate friendships and mutual support of these "cultured people." ৯

# Tea: Tung Ting Oolong

Taiwan (Formosa) teas are large-leaf teas, and are processed in an exceptionally wide range of moisture-to-leaf content, giving it its singular floral fragrance and taste that has no duplicate anywhere. One of the special ones is Tung Ting, a greenish oolong, with its leaves often rolled into a small ball. The pleasure of drinking this tea begins with a slight astringent taste of green that segues into a smooth floral trip on the tongue. The sensation is nearly intoxicating because of the embracing combination of heady fragrance and rich taste. Buy fresh, use quickly, buy again. Brew one teaspoon of leaves with five ounces of water if using a conventional teapot and cups. Completely decant the liquor after brewing. Begin by brewing this tea for thirty seconds to a minute, and longer to taste. The leaves should offer several intense servings.

*On a small straw mat the*
*summer moon is reflected*
*in a tea kettle.*

—Issa (1763–1827)

# *Tea: Matcha*

The finest quality *matcha*, the brilliant chartreuse green powdered tea of the *chanoyu*, is made from the best quality green tea of Japan, Gyokuro. Matcha is prepared by placing a very small amount, about one-quarter to one-half teaspoon of tea, in a wide, flat-bottomed bowl, adding some hot water, about four ounces, then whisking the mixture with a bamboo whisk into a frothy drink that is both bitter and sweet. It goes well with red bean (*azuki*) cakes and similar Japanese sweets or dark chocolate.

As an alternative, consider a high-grade Japanese green Spiderleg or the dew-sweet Gyokuro. Japanese green teas are readily available in Japanese grocery stores and, of course, online. Choose tightly packaged teas and look for the expiration date to ensure freshness. Matcha should be refrigerated between uses.

MEDITATION 11

*At One with Nature*

To stand at the edge of the sea . . . is to have knowledge
of things that are as eternal as any earthly life can be.

—Rachel Carson (1907–1964)

Adjectives were probably invented to describe the splendor of the natural world. Who has not spilled countless words to describe the rising and setting of the sun, the majesty of mountains and trees, the rhythm of water from ponds to oceans, and all the other flora, fauna, and beauty in between? To view even a humble herb garden or a flurry of daisies in the side yard is still a measure of the magic of our world.

Anyone who hikes or watches birds, picnics or rides a horse, or plays tourist among the marvels of this earth, has experienced meditative moments. Awe is no casual feeling, and there is so much of nature that continues to conjure awe in us.

Memories from my childhood in southwest Pennsylvania include the taste of the water spilling through the rocky mountain walls near the Braddock Memorial, and the squishy-slimy feel of my first lake swim and the summer nights lit by fireflies echoed forever by the constellations.

Living in Los Angeles, where the stars are standing next to you in the checkout line at Whole Foods and electric lights cloud the moon, it is way too easy to forget the everyday wonders. Yet just thirty minutes away, in any direction, we can view the powerful ocean, or hike several magnificent mountain ranges; with a little more time and energy, we can camp in glorious state parks, high or low deserts.

My letters to friends during my first few years living in Sausalito were filled with stories about seals splashing toward shore seeking food, seeing Mars from the rooftop of the houseboat, and how the moon and the stars seemed to be lowered onto the visual edge of Richardson Bay as if by a stage manager tugging on a pulley. No matter how many times I walked the Tennessee Valley Trail, glancing at the trail's end—where two mountain ridges stand like curtains closing in on the ocean—always took my breath away.

Returning to Los Angeles for a while, I basked in the warming sun and the pink-blue strokes of sunsets that are particular to this city. Alas, the green plants on the patio were my only real view; seeing the sun required not only walking outside the apartment, but down the street. Fortunately at the end of the block was a pretty park—quiet, isolated, with one magnificent oak tree. Sometimes you have to travel to see nature; sometimes you just have to open your front door. No matter. The point is to seek it out.

How does nature call to you? Are there local public gardens or new trails you have always wanted to explore? Would strolling along the lake or picnicking in the park be your idea of a great way to wind down for an afternoon? Think of someplace near you that you either have not been to since "can't remember when" or that you have been meaning to visit but have not made the time to do it. Make it your next destination.

## Don't Just Sit There, Sit "Out There"

TOMORROW, why not pack up a thermos of your favorite tea, grab a small blanket or pillow, and head out to the sea, the hills, the fields. Take a camera or binoculars or a magnifying glass. Use them to see, really see, the kaleidoscope of patterns, colors, movements in the grass and flowers and, yes, even the bugs, around you. When you

> *Silence is the best response to mystery.*
>
> —Kathleen Norris (b. 1947), American poet and farmer

look at things this closely, you are able to enter other worlds and come back to your own, marveling that you are both on the periphery and totally immersed in the same universal experience called life.

Immersing yourself in the beauty of nature is certainly a treat for the eyes and a balm for the mind. Spend the time at your personal spot just sitting, welcoming meditation at its most sublime. Breathe in deeply, and repeat these deep breaths until you feel your body floating into the surroundings. Observe colors. Revel in the scents that make this place special to you, perhaps the sweetness of flowers or the grasses in the meadow; the bite of the ocean air, the earthy aroma of sand or dirt or fallen leaves. Feel the breezes hug you. Hug back. Open up your arms in welcome. Memorize your feelings to recall them during other meditations.

## Ichigo ichie

*Every encounter is once in a lifetime.*

—Sen Sôshitsu XV (b. 1923)

Before you pack up to return home, allow the symphony of sounds to envelop you. Can you hear the flutter of the wings of birds above you or the whisper of blades of grass? What other sounds can you hear? How do they make you feel? Nothing restores like the drama of natural beauty, from a gorgeous view at your back deck to a trek through canyons and national parks. Even if you are far away from a spot of green, try to live among plants, flowers, herbs. If you do not have room for even a window box, hang a painting or photograph of your favorite vista of nature. It will calm you, remind you of this tender spot in the world, and make you smile.

*One should drink tea while appreciating the fragrance of flowers,*
*the brightness of the moon, the beauty of music. After drinking tea*
*one will no longer be in a daze but feel as frank and as open*
*as heaven and earth.*

—Attributed to the Tang Dynasty Chinese monk
Seng-Jiao Ran (720–799)

# Tea: Qiman (Keemun), the "Burgundy of Teas"

Qiman (Keemun) is a hearty black tea from China with a sweet, fruity edge that is very satisfying. This is a black tea that is stimulating and refreshing and gives great energy to the body, a perfect tea to serve hot or iced, rich and smooth and full-bodied. You can savor it out-of-doors on your ventures or in front of your favorite houseplants or photographs from your trip to the Grand Canyon. Drinking this life-affirming tea respectfully is not unlike viewing the pearls of nature. Brew like you ordinarily brew a black tea, with about a level teaspoon of leaves to five ounces of underboiling water for a minute, taste, brew longer as desired. This tea experience offers a soft, round, full mouth flavor with lingering aftertaste.

*The Chinese Sage Lu Yu described the three levels of heated water in charming ways. The first is "sound distinguishing," when the tiniest bubbles start to appear; the second is "air distinguishing" because steam is occurring, and the third is "form distinguishing" because the placid look of the water has changed form into a plethora of bubbles.*

# Tea: Mint Tea

Mint tea is the national beverage in Morocco, where a footed table is always set in readiness with small glasses and a towering teapot with an elongated spout so that dexterous servers can pour the tea while standing up. In Morocco, mint tea is usually a Chinese green gunpowder, so named because it is rolled into tiny pellets associated with the size and shape of ammunition. In truth the pellets were shaped to preserve freshness and today are still rolled by hand in many areas of China. Gunpowder is a crisp, clean green tea and takes well to the addition of either classic spearmint or true mint. Brew according to the vendor's directions or to taste, and as it steeps, add a mint leaf or two. Strain leaves of both tea and mint, then serve. Sugar may be added if desired. This is a marvelous tea for urban or rural hikers; it's refreshing, thirst quenching, and restores the balance of body fluids after an arduous workout or time spent in the heat of a humid summer day.

MEDITATION 12

# Inviting Love and Peace into the World

Listen to the stillness of you,

My dear, among it all;

I feel your silence touch my words as I talk,

And take them in thrall.

—D. H. Lawrence (1885–1930)

*S*omeone once remarked to my uncle Joe and aunt Mollie that they didn't talk too much with each other. They looked at each other and smiled, then Joe said, "We don't need to. After all this time, we know what we're thinking." And so they did.

Stepping into the silence of each other is part of the deepening of love between mates, between parents and children, between friends. The more we share and reveal, the longer we support and give to one another, the more the bond of true communication strengthens. In time, a certain gesture can say what entire monologues can attempt; we develop a shorthand glossary of words and phrases that catapult us to memories that make us laugh or swoon.

Can meditations with tea help you find and keep the love of your life? Can they help create and sustain a happy family life? Can they cement friendships? I believe the answer is *yes*. Of course they work best, as life works best, when your heart is kind, your mind is open, and your goal is joy for others. For venerable tea masters, harmony is part of a proper attitude toward tea. From drinking tea, one can apply harmony to how we live with one another; how we work, conducting ourselves ethically and graciously; being charitable and receptive to the views of others, even if they differ from our own.

Can you do this constantly? Probably not, but do not despair. Only saints and martyrs live a perfectly loving life, acting perfectly every moment of the day. You and I are human. We get cranky when we're blue or ill, we lash out when we get hurt, we disregard the feelings of others in favor of our own, we rush past obligations in pursuit of desires. And, yet—if we try, even occasionally, to slow down, think of how to demonstrate our love for family and friends, we will be more loving—and more lovable.

*The only lasting beauty is the beauty of the heart.*
*Love is the energizing elixir of the universe, the cause*
*and effect of all harmonies.*

—Rumi

## Consider Peace

THE ROMAN EMPEROR Cicero complained that "children were not obeying their parents, and everyone is writing a book"—additional evidence that the more things change the more they stay the same. Yet this is a time when fear, mistrust, and the scourges of unfamiliar disease and dilemmas are shaking our beliefs. How can we invite peace into such a world? How can we ensure health? How could we find love? The answers are legion, but it is my feeling that everything begins with the idea that each individual is in charge of her/his own life. That's damn hard to be in a war zone, or in a territory with no agriculture or money to import food, or in a culture where the freedom to think is curtailed by a despotic, controlling government. It's even hard to be when you live in America, living paycheck to paycheck, worried about losing the job, the health insurance, the gossamer feeling of belonging to a community of workers.

So where to begin? A peaceful world begins with people who respect harmony over discord, who value accomplishment through effort over possession by terror or theft. To reach that apex, people must cherish some time to be quiet over the constancy of numbing cacophony. They must treasure moments alone as much as companionship with others, and love their friends and family more than they could ever hate anyone else. If you have attempted a few of the meditations or yogalike exercises described in this book, and you have begun to view tea as a form of quiet luxury, you are on your way to carving out a calm nook in your own life, and a sure path of peaceful existence no matter what the world around you is like.

Extending the peace to your neighborhood is the next step. What are the challenges that face your block? Your condo complex? Your extended community? What solutions can you come up with? You have vats of untapped imagination—we all do—so dip into that storehouse to pull up some ingenious and long-ranging answers to those challenges.

# Looking Out for One Another

*To meditate does not mean to fight with a problem.*
*To meditate means to observe.*
*Your smile proves it. It proves that you are being gentle*
*with yourself that the sun of awareness is shining in you,*
*that you have control of your situation.*
*You are yourself, and you have acquired some peace.*

—Thich Nhat Hanh (Thây)

MANY AN ARCHITECT and homeowner has rued the declining use of porches or verandas along the front of family homes. They were the perfect spot to rest, nod to passersby, invite neighbors or friends to stop a while to chat or refresh themselves with tea or lemonade. Today, even in the coziest of neighborhoods, it is rare to have neighbors who are friendly (much less friends), and in some cases, they are indifferent to our lives or our safety. Having a deck in the back of the house may be a nice way to relax and enjoy our gardens, but it further isolates us, giving us privacy when what many of us need is community. Fortunately, there are many ways to look out for one another. In neighborhoods, we can stage seasonal block parties to introduce ourselves; buddy up and establish phone trees to call one another during crises of bad weather or catastrophes like fire, and best of all, we may make friends to enjoy throughout the year. In our own circle of intimates and friends, calling or visiting is critical to ensuring that isolation and loneliness do not cloak our friends. Email is loads of fun, but the sound of a familiar voice, the inflection that shows concern, the tone that says someone cares are infinitely important, and a blessing for both. Look around your neighborhood—perhaps in a condominium building, or an apartment house. Is there someone who could use an uplifting phone call or a weekly visit from you? Is there someone with whom you've been too busy to sustain a friendship and you could reestablish ties? Is there a family member who has grown apart from you that could be re-involved in your immediate family's gatherings? Reach out. Embrace. Involve yourself in the welfare of someone else. The richness and joy that will come back to you will be astonishing.

## Sharing What We Know

How would introducing meditation with tea impact at-risk youth in your area? Could you teach them the benefits you have learned? Could you share the pleasures of tea drinking with a cola generation? Start with your own children, nieces or nephews, their friends, children of friends. Invite them for a casual tea. Ask them what they need or want to make their mark in the world. Sometimes, extending a hand as a mentor or information source is all that is necessary to turn a conflicted youth onto the rightful path.

# Changing How We Look Outward

ANGER. JEALOUSY. Hostility. Hate. How do these feelings enter our consciousness and why? No human being has lived without experiencing some of these feelings, even if we know that feeling or expressing them can make us less than what we can be. But we can be angry about the inequity of justice in the world and turn that anger into action. We can be jealous of what others do or have, and use that to fuel our work toward what we desire. We can hate and in doing so, we destroy, or we can recognize that we must relook at those we hate with empathy and compassion; to identify some trait, some characteristic to respect—and do what we can to help them discover something to respect in us. We can begin at home, at work, in the community, then in the world at large, one step at a time, or perhaps, as Sen Sôshitsu XV would have it, over a bowl of tea.

*Seek spiritual riches within. What you are is much greater than anyone or anything else you have ever yearned for.*

—Paramahansa Yogananda (1893–1952)

## MEDITATION ON COMPASSION

One of the benefits of meditations is being so in touch with oneself that we learn to "make friends with" the good and the not-so good qualities that are in all of us. We may not verbalize it, but pettiness, jealousy, anger, or other feelings—rooted in hurt—exist in all of us in some measure. By inviting compassion and understanding into our minds and hearts—for ourselves—we can achieve not perfection, but genuine acceptance of everything that we are. When we accept who and what we are, we are on the road to accepting other people, other cultures, and ideas. How can this acceptance be achieved?

Perhaps anger is your "not-so-good" trait. When you want to beat up on yourself because you are angry about something you did or did not do, remind yourself to stop and ask yourself, "Why am I angry in the first place?" If you want to beat someone else up because you are angry about something he did, absolutely stop and ask yourself why you have this feeling. "What is it he is doing that hurts me so? What is the benefit of such anger?" The more you practice recognizing when you're entering the "anger mode" the sooner you will be better able to ask yourself hard questions about why you feel this anger. Does it bring up memories of hurt or helplessness from previous experiences? Does such action spotlight that you are not "perfect," even though you may realize perfection is an ideal, not a reality? Is this how your family "taught" you to respond to similar situations?

The obligation you have to yourself is to channel the energy of hateful anger into the positive energy of kindness to your whole being. Do you feel yourself shutting down, hardening your heart, turning away from others? *Don't go there.* Instead, open up your heart as much as you can. Soften enough to allow kindness in. Be compassionate with yourself. Practice loving kindness to yourself. As you practice, so it shall be. Remember, this is not a prayer for change, it is a meditation on *acceptance* by truly wishing to know happiness and the root of happiness, peace and the root of peace, love and the root of love in you, and in others.

## The Four Limitless Qualities

East Indian and other Asian meditation practices have many overlapping ideas. The following are four that I believe are universal, in one form or another, in most cultures. Adopt them as you wish.

**Maitri:** May I, and all beings, enjoy happiness and the root of happiness.

**Compassion:** May I, and all beings, be free from suffering and the root of suffering.

**Joy:** May I, and all beings, never be separated from the great happiness devoid of suffering.

**Equanimity:** May I, and all beings, dwell in the great equanimity, free from aggression and prejudice.

Practice this meditation for yourself first. Then you can move to meditation of these qualities for those you love, for those you do not know, for those you consider an enemy, and finally for all beings.

*Maitri* is a form of kindness meditation. *Maitri*, a Sanskrit word adopted by the Buddhist monks Chögyam Trungpa Rinpoche and Suzuki Roshi, is based on the idea that by offering "unconditional friendliness" to ourselves we can transform ourselves, and in turn transform the world around us.

This is not to be confused with "self-help" or "self-improvement." In *self-acceptance* of all of our qualities, in "befriending who we are already" as Pema Chödrön, an American Buddhist nun, has posited, is the belief that both "our neurosis and our wisdom are part of who we are. As we make friends, so to speak, with our neurosis, we can be gentle enough with ourselves to observe it, learn from it and, if possible, let it go." In this exercise of lovingkindness to ourselves, we can learn that the anger and jealousy and hate we observe in ourselves is based on hurt. Only then can we make the first tentative steps toward developing the compassion needed to make understanding—and accepting—of ourselves and others in the world a reality. Compassion in the world begins with *you*.

*The heart that enters the Way is the best teacher.*

—Rikyû

## Tea: Lu'an Melon Tea

I dream about this tea. Even though the memory of its delicate melon sweetness is ten years old now, it was the tea that irrevocably changed how I thought of tea. It awakened the palate to the variety and scope of what lay ahead. Memory can be cruel, in a way, because no lu'an I have tasted since has come close to the ambrosial melon aftertaste of that first adventure (but the detours have been just as exciting). Sometimes referred to as melon seeds or Lu'an Gua Pian, it is delicate, sweet, pale green to yellow, like liquid honeydew. This green tea, one of the most popular in Mainland China, is grown in the Anhui province and made solely from just one particular leaf atop the tea bush. Exquisite. Special. Memorable. Brew lightly and reinfuse as desired.

> *The first cup should have a haunting flavor,*
> *strange and lasting.*
>
> —Lu Yu

## Tea: Ginger Peach

Ginger, which is a root full of magical health properties, is a powerful aid to digestion. Its sharp tang is an intriguing contrast to the soft velvet taste of peach. Putting them together in a rich black Nilgiri or Assam black tea is a triumphant triumvirate of blending. Many packaged teas offer this delightful combination. To make your own, add a thin slice of fresh gingerroot and a slice of dried peach to some boiling water, then lower the heat and simmer for one to two minutes longer. Strain out the gingerroot and peach and pour the water over dried tea leaves or teabags; steep according to the vendor's directions or to taste. Strain out leaves and serve. Excellent after a hearty meal. You'll never celebrate a Thanksgiving Day feast without it again.

*The monks of the Chinese Cha'n sect of Buddhists believed that the first cup of tea helped to keep a calm and clear mind while they sat in meditation. The second cup helped them feel as if the spirit was cleansed by gentle rain. After a third cup, one can understand the nature of things.*

—Anecdotal saying

# Tea: Ceylon

Black teas from Sri Lanka, known as Ceylon teas after the country's former name, are varied in taste, from lightly brisk to heavily rich. For the best, opt for selections from the regions of Uva, Dimbulla, or Kandy. Ceylon teas brew up to a golden liquor in the cup, and have a light flowery fragrance and delicate taste with just a hint of astringency. Delicious alone or with lemon. Although plain Ceylon teas take to milk well, their delicacy shines through readily when drunk plain. Brew with one teaspoon to five ounces of under-boiling water for two minutes, taste, then brew longer as desired.

# Sustaining the Benefits of Meditations with Tea

*The spiritual journey is individual, highly personal. It can't be organized or regulated. It isn't true that everybody should follow one path. Listen to your own truth.*

—Ram Dass (b. 1931)

Now that you have had a glimpse of the benefits of bringing meditations with tea into your life, I hope you will bless yourself with them many many times in the future. Do it when you want to, do it when you need to, and always meditate and prepare tea with intent, for the body—and the tea—*knows*.

As much satisfaction as I have received from these experiences, neither meditation nor tea is an absolutely, positively, everyday thing with me. Still, if I go longer than two days without it, I feel jangled, and sit right down where I am to rest, recuperate, relax in a meditative moment, and always come away totally refreshed.

This practice has made all of my life richer, deeper, more real. Whenever you find yourself in situations that make you uncomfortable, when you are stuck in traffic or waiting on line, or worried about important meetings, think back. Recall the best moments you have had in meditation practice. Conjure up those feelings and let them strengthen you.

Sometimes, even now, meditation can cause sorrow to rise, yet just as drinking tea can wash away sorrow, the tears of remembrance of griefs past, can wear away at the pain. Meditation sharpens my focus, builds up my foundation of strength of purpose, and steers me in the right direction for this moment in my life. It calms and energizes just like tea does.

The goal of this book is not to lead you to the life of an aesthete, a monk or nun, or a hermit. The goal was, and always will be, to give you some ideas of how meditations with tea can help you live your life in a fuller way, so that you can pursue your dreams and wishes.

*Learn to do good,*
*Cease to do harm,*
*Control the mind,*
*And benefit others.*
—Objectives of Buddhist behavior

## Keep Breathing!

TO LEARN about breathing exercises, take a class with a yoga instructor, particularly one who teaches Kundalini or Iyengar yoga. Accredited instructors in the Alexander Technique or Pilates will help you become more aware of how breathing affects your body while sitting, walking, or lying down. Join a choir or take singing lessons. Take ballet or modern dance. All of these disciplines recognize the importance of "the breath" and how it helps us physically and mentally to use the oxygen so critical to our health. Take a class in particular meditation techniques, from Transcendental Meditation to Buddhist, or attend a retreat connected with your spiritual center, church, or synagogue. Stretching your mind and your body is empowering, enriching, and strengthening in ways that can astonish you.

## Keep Walking!

DOG OWNERS may rue the obligation of walking their pet once or twice a day, but, truly, the walk gains the owner more benefits than those gained by the dog.

Hike to see the beauty of nature and stretch those legs. You'll build up lung power, and be reminded of the wonder of sea, sand, or mountains at the same time.

Park your car farther away from your destination and walk to it. Explore your neighborhood by foot; look for the prettiest routes and walk them often. Walk to the nearest mailbox instead of driving to the post office. Walk outside the office and explore the neighborhood on foot. Look at people and their infinite variety. Look for patches of flowers and shading trees. These brief walking breaks will add powerful mini meditations to your day, giving you energy and alertness.

## Walk a Labyrinth!

BOTH PRIVATE AND PUBLIC labyrinths are being built all over the country now with many others being built every day in backyards, in public parks, churches and synagogues, and private and public venues. When traveling, seek out public labyrinths to defuse jet lag or stress. For locations, see the resources list in the back of this book.

*Silence is the element in which great things fashion themselves.*

—Maurice Maeterlinck (1862–1949), Belgian author

# Drink Tea!

- Experiment.
- Go beyond the familiar.
- Imagine you're the Marco (or Mary) Polo of tea and explore this world.
- If you prefer tea bags, opt for ones containing better grades of tea.
- Try loose-leaf tea at least once in your life. No need for fancy equipment, just two cups and a strainer.
- If you always drink black, try an oolong. If you've tasted greens, you're ready for a white. If you prefer scented or fruited teas, try at least one tea "plain." Buy organic whenever possible.

## 1-2-3 TEA PREPARATION

1. Put loose-leaf tea in a cup.
2. Fill the cup with hot water to infuse.
3. Pour the infused liquor through a strainer into the second cup.

It is that simple, and the tea will definitely taste better than what you make with a teabag that's been stuck on the grocer's shelf for ages.

For a glimpse at the plethora of teas available at tea shops and at the grocery store, see the resources in the back of this book. Order online, mail order, make a phone order or walk into the local tea merchant and ask questions. For specifics about tea, read on!

# Tea: The Simplicity of Leaf and Water

*Tea is naught but this: First you heat the water, then you make the tea, then you drink it properly. That is all you need to know.*

—Rikyû

There is an old Fujian saying, *Chaye xue dao lao, chaye micheng xue bu liao*. "Even though one studies tea until old age, one can never learn all the names of types of tea." That, fortunately, hardly stops anyone who discovers the pure pleasure of this simple leaf brewed with water. One can indeed spend a lifetime exploring the world of tea, and I hope you do! You could try something exotic like an Assam white or a Darjeeling oolong; you could sip *lu'an*, the tea that tastes like summer melon; or drink a *fukamushi cha*, a Japanese sweet green tea that, like all fine teas, relaxes and enervates at the same time.

As mentioned earlier, the one absolutely remarkable fact is that all true tea comes from the same plant, the *Camellia sinensis* (Chinese camellia), a single evergreen shrub that is a botanical relative of the flowering camellia bush. It grows in subtropical climates, usually at high or very high altitudes, and its leaves make what we now call tea. Tea grows in more than thirty-five countries, and altitude, humidity, the care and attention of the farmer, and the weather whims of Mother Nature all contribute to the health, and the flavor, of the leaves.

Although machine plucking is not uncommon, most quality tea is still hand-plucked in many areas, primarily by women and young girls, except in Kenya where the men do the plucking. Even when done by hand, plucking can be cavalier, with workers grabbing handfuls of the top leaves, or a whole slew of branches. In contrast, the most sought-after leaves are the top three, the leaf bud and the top two leaves, known as pekoe and orange pekoe. Careful pluckers accomplish this by using the middle finger and thumb. The word "pekoe," then, is related to a leaf size, not a flavor or a process (one of the many misleading words in the intriguing world of tea).

Tea leaves are visually fascinating, with nearly endless choices. Tea leaves can be rolled into pellets, shaped into long twists, curled into ribbons, even woven together to resemble fruits, flowers, or even hummingbirds' nests. The leaves can be dried whole, broken, or pulverized.

Why are the flavors so different? The answer is two-fold: place of origin (geography, weather, varietal), and style of processing.

## Processing

PROCESSING is all about leaf and water. Rain feeds the plants, supplemented by water given by the farmer. After the leaves are picked, they are spread out on very long drying racks—sometimes sixty feet long—to air dry. Then, depending on how the leaves will be processed, water is removed through some form of oxidation: either by sun or air, by temperature-controlled heat in roasting bins, or by the most primitive (yet totally workable) method, in stone woks heated by fire. Processors move their hands throughout the woks to make sure the leaves are evenly dried, an artful skill honed after years of practice. The final water and leaf step occurs when your tea leaves infuse in hot water, providing your cup of pleasure.

Like wine, what makes teas taste so different from one another, along with where they have grown and when they are plucked, is how they are processed.

For many years, the process of drying leaves has erroneously been called "fermentation." The correct term is "oxidation," for the processing of tea is not unlike the oxidation that occurs when a cut apple or pear is left out in the air and dries slightly, then turns brown.

The balance of tea and water is what tea is all about. When the teas are plucked (picked), they are flexible and green, reflecting their moisture content. The leaves are then oxidized to alter their water content slightly, either to shape them and/or to give them a specific taste that can only be achieved through this process.

Some leaves are lightly steamed to retain their intense green color and sweet flavor, others are dried by air, or sun-dried.

**Yellow** teas are quite rare. Once offered solely as tribute teas reserved for royalty or esteemed guests, some stellar examples have found their way to the U.S., and are highly prized. Both the leaves and the infusion are pale yellow in color and are very delicate and made from buds only. Brewed, they are pale sage or yellow or even without color. Their processing and flavor are similar to those of green tea, but the taste is usually softer, mellower than the grassy flavor profile of most greens.

Prime yellow teas come from the Sichuan Province; although quite rare, seek out Meng-ding Huang Ya, a tea of legendary flavor. It grows atop the "heavenly country" of Mount Meng. Another one to look for is Jun Shan Yin Zhen, purportedly the favored tea of Chairman Mao, who demanded only the finest.

*Knock on your inner door and no other.*

—Rumi

**White** tea leaves are not exactly white, but rather the palest sage in color. Unlike black or oolong teas, white teas are not oxidized at all, but may be withered to make them flexible enough to shape them into various styles. The flavor of whites ranges from nearly ephemeral to lightly sweet; they brew in the cup to a pale or dark sage, or yellow, although no color in the cup is common. Elegant, beautiful in their form, they lend themselves to a glass or clear vessel to give tea lovers a little drama. Often called "senior tea" in China, the lower caffeine content makes white teas good for older people or for those who want just a little caffeine.

**Green** teas range from deep hunter green to pale yellow/green. They can be vegetal in flavor from an intensely grassy characteristic to a subtle taste. Redolent of asparagus, spinach, or similar greens, green teas are lightly steamed, retaining the fresh green taste and color of the leaf. Brewed, they can be nearly colorless or sage-green, light yellow to light green. The finest greens from China are delicate, the best from Japan have a richer chlorophyll sweetness, and Sri Lanka (Ceylon) greens, particularly the organic varieties, are assertive, clean, and very refreshing.

*Note*: Both whites and greens are brewed quite cool, 170–185° F or lower and have a range of tastes that is extraordinarily wide, from slightly sweet or grassy to more intense variations.

**Oolong** teas are neither one hundred percent oxidized like blacks, nor completely un-oxidized like whites or greens. Instead, they have the widest range of oxidation—from two to eighty percent. The leaves can be greenish to nearly black, and often appear to be green in the center with brown edges, reflecting the limited oxidation. The greenest oolongs are referred to as *pouchongs* and taste similarly to greens, yet with the distinctive floral note that is signature to oolongs. The liquors are rich gold and red-gold, and the most popular ones are Formosa Oolong, Tung Ting, and Ti Kwan Yin. Oolongs come from Taiwan (Formosa) and the Fujian province of mainland China. Oolongs are brewed at temperatures from 185–190°F, usually using an abundance of leaves to small quantities of water, to bring out the intensity of flavor. The brew in the cup varies from golden to darker tones.

**Black** teas are familiar to most people, and they are the teas typically found in packaged blends such as Irish or English Breakfast. Most Assams, Qimans (Keemuns), and Ceylons are fully oxidized, resulting in brewed teas with a spectrum of beautiful liquors from golden orange, to red orange, to mahogany. The Chinese call these teas red to reflect the color in the cup, although Westerners call them black because the complete one hundred percent oxidation results in leaves that appear black in color.

The world's best-quality teas are grown in India, Taiwan (Formosa), Sri Lanka (Ceylon), China, and Japan. Based on topography, altitude, weather, and of course, processing, each has a certain flavor profile or characteristics that sets it apart from the others. Teas from Ceylon and India tend to be crisp, clean, "brisk"; those from Japan and China tend to be delicate and sweet (in the sense that butter lettuce is sweeter than romaine); and Taiwan teas have a distinctive heady floral scent and taste, although the variables to all of these teas are fantastic. Following are the most popular or commonly known examples of teas from each of these primary growing areas. Technically, any tea could be processed as a white, yellow, green, oolong, black or *pu-erh*, but custom, style, history, and market demand govern the chosen processing methods.

# China Teas

THE HOMELAND of tea, China offers teas touched with poetry, from their names—"spring jade" or "after the rain"—to flavors that range from hearty to ephemeral, with no end of variety. Among their offerings are:

**White:** White teas like Silver Needle, a long, elegant, pale-sage leaf, are popularly served in highball glasses where the leaves dance downward or float gracefully in cups. Other favorites are Shou Mei and Pai Mutan (peony flowers).

**Green:** The greens, from the rolled Gunpowder or the delicate leaf Pi Lo Chun or Young Hysons and others are exceptional in their sweetness and light color. Lung Ching or Dragonwell is the most prized of green teas and has upwards of seven grades.

**Oolong:** Mainland China offers large-leaf oolongs, with Ti Kwan Yin the most famous.

**Black:** Richly aromatic selections like Keemun and Yunnan are certainly among the most popular, and Yunnan is also processed as a green.

**Pu-erh:** In some Chinese provinces, nearly every person drinks a bedtime cup of pu-erh, an intentionally aged tea that can be made from teas processed as green, oolong or black. The original style of processing (green, oolong or black) manages to come through despite the age of the pu-erhs which can be from several months to fifty years or longer. Its earthy, deep flavor makes pu-erh a popular digestive as has been jokingly referred to as "Chinese penicillin."

**Jasmine:** Although some black teas are scented with these intoxicating flowers, the finest Chinese jasmine teas are made with green tea leaves, providing a delicate, faintly aromatic experience that is incredible. The liquor brews up lightly green and the fragrance lingers for quite a while. The tea is scented by placing jasmine flowers on beds of tea leaves overnight because the flower only blooms at night. The layering is repeated several times until the tea leaves are infused with the jasmine scent. The use of jasmine oils or artificial flavorings may heighten the aroma, but they also alter the taste considerably, so beware! Instead of a cocktail, have a luxurious tea with a heady, intoxicating scent, like a jasmine.

# India Teas

INDIA OFFERS a remarkable variety of teas, from well-balanced Nilgiris to the delicately fragrant Darjeelings, the rich, hearty Assams, and many more.

**Assam:** Although there have been some uniquely processed white ones, and an infrequent good green one, basically Assam is processed as black and is the strong soldier of tea, hearty, fragrant, and able to stand up beautifully to milk. An ideal tea for blending with those teas that need a little punch, it brews up to a golden or red gold liquor. It is grown not from the small Chinese variety of *Camellia sinensis* that is used for teas in nearby Darjeeling but from the larger-leaf *Camellia assamica*, which originated in the wilds of the forests in the state of Assam.

**Darjeeling:** Home to fewer than eighty farms, this region of northeast India stands facing the awesome Himalayas, and some say the mystique of the mountains permeates the tea leaves with a distinctive delicate yet sharp fragrance matched with a taste that is, when properly brewed, simply divine. Darjeeling is the most prized, and most expensive, tea produced in India. While only two percent of India tea is grown in Darjeeling, the income produced by it is often higher than the total from the rest of the country's tea production. This despite the fact that the number of tea estates has dwindled to fewer than eighty from a high of one hundred and eight only twenty years ago. Darjeelings have been processed many ways, as whites, greens, or oolongs but usually as blacks. A celebratory type of tea, it has been referred to as the champagne of teas. Its liquor ranges from golden yellow to golden red, and its bouquet and taste often conjure up peaches, apricots, or nectarines. Darjeelings are direct descendants of the Chinese *jat* or Chinese *Camellia sinensis*, although they do not taste like China teas. Darjeelings taste like stone fruit due to the altitude in which they are grown, like the continuing mist, like the Himalayas. . . .

**Nilgiri:** These exceptional black teas are known as Blue Mountain teas, in reference to the Nilgiri mountain range, which from some distance indeed looks blue. Nilgiri teas are wonderful, clean-tasting, and soft—an excellent choice for a stand-alone tea. Previously relegated to blending status, Nilgiri teas have evolved into better quality, color, and taste. They brew a liquor that is a golden color with a sweet fragrance, excellent for iced tea because it does not cloud and takes to fruits and flavorings exceptionally well.

## Japanese Teas

JAPAN has only recently embraced British-style black teas served with milk and American-style iced black teas, yet it is green tea that is most popular throughout this small island. Highly prized at home, the finest Japanese green teas are rarely exported, but good examples of Japanese teas can be found throughout the U.S. They include:

**Matcha,** the powdered green tea used in the Japanese tea ceremony. It has a slightly bitter brew despite its sweet frothiness. It is only and always made from fine Gyokuro tea leaves that have been steamed, dried, then crushed and powdered into a brilliant chartreuse color. It is not steeped, but whisked with hot water for thick or thin tea for *chanoyu* (the tea ceremony of Japan). *Matcha* is made in many grades, and pricing indicates the rank of quality. Some organic *matcha* is available.

**Sencha,** the most commonly drunk green tea in Japan and often referred to as everyday tea, is lightly steamed or dried and hand processed to preserve its delicate, grassy green taste. Many grades are available. Good quality *sencha* should taste and smell grassy sweet.

**Spiderleg** is a style of green tea with long willowy twisted leaves, and it comes in a wide range of quality. It unfurls beautifully and elegantly in the cup, making it a visual delight.

**Gyokuro** is the most highly prized of Japanese green teas. Its intense green color and heightened sweet taste is the result of covering the leaves for extended periods of time to slow photosynthesis and increase the flavor elements. Sometimes referred to as Precious Dew.

**Genmaicha** is a popular green tea blended with small popped corn and bits of toasted barley or rice. It is roasty, sweetish, and delicious with food.

**Houjicha** is a roasted green tea with a mild nutty flavor, excellent with most cuisines, and a good green tea for anyone new to green teas or Japanese teas.

# Sri Lanka (Ceylon) Teas

SRI LANKA recaptured its traditional name, but the teas that grow on this beautiful island still fall under the name of *Ceylon*, which was popularized by the great teaman and advertising genius, Sir Thomas Lipton. The most delightful of these teas are from such tea-growing areas as Nuwara Eliya, Dimbulla, Ratnapura, Uwa, and Kandy. Most brew up to reddish-orange liquors of various strengths, and have the slightly astringent, clean taste that Sir Lipton dubbed "brisk" with good reason. They have a wonderfully aromatic fragrance that signifies Sri Lanka teas. Sri Lanka has become a pioneer in the emerging category of fine organic teas.

# Taiwan (Formosa) Teas

FORMOSA, now known as a part of the People's Republic of China or Taiwan, is an island right across the water from the Fujian Province in mainland China that produces excellent oolongs, the most famous being Ti Kwan Yin. Many oolong lovers challenge that the Formosa oolong is the finest in the world. While many grades of Formosa oolongs exist, reflecting the quality of processing, they all share a very wonderful golden red to red liquor and the better ones give off a pungent, sweet aroma like no other. It is important to buy and use these teas soon after processing; they keep only for several weeks or a few months at most. A subcategory called *pouchong* give a lighter green to greenish-yellow cup and have a green taste profile reflecting their shorter processing times.

# Favorite Blends and Tea "Drinks"

**Breakfast Blends:** Irish and English are the most typical breakfast blends, with Irish being the stronger of the two. Usually, but not always, each contains black China teas with or without Indian black Assam or African Kenya.

**Chai:** This tea drink of India is brewed in milk with a mélange of spices ranging from pepper to cardamom to cinnamon. The proper name is *masala chai*, because *chai* literally means "tea," so to say "chai tea" actually means to say "tea tea." Often, a lower-quality, fully dried black tea is used in the making of *masala chai*, which is cooked for a long time and served in India from backpack samovars or large thermos vats by street tea vendors called *chaiwallas*, who seem to be at every train stop or bazaar, offering a bit of nourishment for pennies. This peppery tea blend is a fixture in North India, but there is growing enthusiasm for brewing it with south Indian teas like Nilgiri.

**Earl Grey:** This is the classic black tea blend with oil of bergamot, a Mediterranean pear-shaped citrus that lends the tea a delightful twist. Twinings Tea of London made and sold the blend for years but, alas, failed to copyright the recipe, although it avers it has the corner on the particular bergamot used in the original blend. That is why one can find various interpretations of the tea blend. It is quite likely that the Chinese orange blossom, the gweifruit or kweifruit, was the original flavoring, but like so many legends of tea, this one, too, may be apocryphal. Earl Grey is, nonetheless, a wonderful afternoon tea, a perfect accompaniment to foods, and refreshing alone. You can find the blend made with lavender, orange, and the familiar bergamot with either Indian or Chinese black teas or blended blacks.

**Thai Tea:** This black tea, usually mixed with condensed milk or coconut milk, is a wonderful complement to the spiciness of many Thai foods. It is usually served iced, but can be heated. The base tea used is of modest quality and the leaves are crushed. Packages of the ground black tea are available at most Thai or other Asian food markets.

**Bubble Tea** is the latest phenomenon of tea drinks, made from tea, milk, sugar, and large black balls of tapioca. The recipes for this "pudding in a cup" are legion, and it is ideal for introducing teens and younger children to tea as a fun drink, one with far less sugar than colas, and containing no additives or harmful chemicals.

## Tea Blossoms with Fragrance

*There are 108 Chinese characters for tea; however, the main one features flowers and grass at the top and wood at the bottom, and man in between, revealing the Chinese concept that balance with nature is achieved completely with tea.*

ALTHOUGH I have been writing about tea for fifteen years, I have yet to discover the perfect word or phrase that describes the wonderful sweet-tangy aroma of fresh tea that greets you when you enter a fine tea shop or, better yet, when you visit a tea manufacturer to view the freshly plucked leaves drying on the long-screened troughs. It is, well, it's the smell of tea!

The aroma of tea leaves does not necessarily match the liquor in the cup; sometimes it is more intense, sometimes less, because of the brewing. After drinking your first cup, the scent will linger for you to inhale, enhancing this totally sensory experience.

You need not have a formal ceremony to enjoy tea. Simply pour a little of your tea into small cups and pass it around to your guests or savor it alone if this is a solo tea experience. The Tea Masters of yore understood that we savor tea with our eyes, our mouths, and, yes, with our nose; all quicken our appetite for a delicious bowl of tea.

## ENHANCING THE NECTAR

*One plum blossom makes the whole world fragrant.*

—Traditional Japanese proverb

While tea is marvelous alone, blending it with flowers and fruits and other aromatic elements not only makes for a delightful range of flavors, it offers an elegant form of aromatherapy, perfect to lead one into a deeper, lasting period of meditation. Blending teas is a time-honored tradition begun centuries ago in China and Japan. The fragrance of flowers helped to deepen the experience with tea, as it enhanced the Victorian language of flowers, too. During that era, sweethearts let the choice of flower send unspoken (yet not unfelt) sentiments to their intended. This charming idea has many applications for your meditation practice and is a wholly natural way to approach it.

The flowers listed below are the most popular ones blended with tea. Most people prefer no distractions of scent or sound when they meditate, yet others believe soft music or delicate fragrance deepens the process. The key word is *delicate*, because both sound and scent should augment, not distract, from the voyage toward your inner self.

If you choose to scent your meditation corner, consider a clean-burning soy candle with a light touch of lavender or rose, or incense made with natural oils from flowers—rather than synthetic perfumes. Both candles and incense contribute to the relaxing spirit of meditation when used discreetly. Commercial incense made in Japan is an excellent choice for premium floral scents because they burn cleanly. Many are specifically made for use in tea ceremonies, so attention is paid to how they will complement the aroma of brewed tea.

> *The ideal lover of flowers is he who visits them in their native*
> *haunts, like Taoyeunming, who sat before a broken bamboo*
> *fence in converse with the wild chrysanthemum, or Linwosing,*
> *losing himself amid mysterious fragrance as he wandered in*
> *the twilight among the plum-blossoms of the Western Lake.*
> *'Tis said that Chowmushih slept in a boat so that his dreams*
> *might mingle with those of the lotus.*

—Okakura Kakuzo

# NIGHT-FLOWERING JASMINE

Certainly, no tea is more famous for its fragrance than jasmine. The flower is a night-bloomer, opening its white petals only after the sun sleeps—when dedicated teamen blanket the green tea with a layer of the fragrant blossom. The tea leaves are infused with jasmine's perfume throughout the night. In the dawn of day, the flowers are removed, and later that night, the entire process is repeated. To achieve the best combination of exquisite aroma and ambrosial taste, the layering process is repeated seven times.

Jasmine is an exceptional conduit for relaxation, particularly if you desire a meditative moment in the early evening or before retiring. The choices for jasmine tea are as beautiful as they are delicious: green leaves rolled into small balls or "pearls"; tiny half-inch *mudans* shaped like hummingbirds' nests, small graceful leaves, and many other choices. For the most effective meditation experience, and for the most satisfying tasting, choose only the finest, freshest jasmine tea, avoiding any that is artificially flavored or colored. (Although black tea is sometimes used in jasmine blends, these are still rare and most are made from either Chinese or Taiwanese greens. If your jasmine looks black and is labeled a green tea, it is too old to drink!) In the language of flowers, jasmine is not unlike its heady, sensual scent, for it says "I'm too happy" or "I attach myself to you" or the "transport of ecstasy," a reference to the luxurious feel of the tea to our other senses. It is not a timid scent, but one that wraps everyone and everything in its intoxicating perfume. Drink it judiciously!

## Chinese Rosebuds

The Chinese have been scenting teas for millennia, and one hugely popular choice is rose *congou*, a black tea scented with the delicacy of tiny pink rosebuds. Small, about three-quarters of an inch long, and of course, food grade, these rosebuds proffer both a light scent and a silky feel to the palate. Rose petals can also be used—their pretty pink color scattered throughout a tin of tea is a painting for the eyes. An infusion of hot water and the rosebuds makes a delicate "intermission" between meals. Beauty, love, grace, all of these are the sentiments that the China rose offers. What beloved does not feel cherished upon receiving a bouquet made from the flower of love?

## LAVENDER

Whether from France, England, or the state of California, lavender is nature's sleeping aid, beautiful to look at, with a smell that is utterly relaxing to breathe in as you prepare for sleep. You can find Earl Grey teas with brilliant lavender petals in place of the traditional bergamot flavor. Consider setting a bouquet of lavender flowers near your meditation corner to blanket the air while you sip tea or meditate.

Because lavender is such a relaxation-inducing flower, you might not want it to scent work areas. But if you keep it primarily in the bedroom or your meditation room, you will help induce sleep. In the language of flowers of the nineteenth century, lavender conveyed a peculiar message, one of mistrust. However, modern-day enthusiasts better understand that lavender is key to the gateway of dreams, relaxation, and deep sleep.

## MINT

In the mint category, primarily true mint or spearmint make a lively addition to tea. Southern iced tea, also known as sweet tea, is frequently served with a decorative sprig of mint that also adds a piquant freshness to the drink. In Morocco, the tea is green and infused with spearmint, poured from tall teapots with elaborately curved spouts that enable the host to stand and theatrically pour the tea into small glasses set on the tea table on the floor. Mint enlivens the palate, therefore, tea made with mint is an excellent aperitif. Mint can also be a digestive when tea with mint is served after meals.

## OSMANTHUS, CITRUS, AND BERGAMOT

The slight acid undercurrent of the Chinese orange blossom, osmanthus; citrus scents from grapefruit to orange or lemon; and the Mediterranean bergamot are ideal for making a transition from a meditative state to the workplace or other activities of the day. Any of these are wonderful flower flavorings for the morning when you are raring to go or for the afternoon when you need a light pick-me-up. Try teas with these scents in brisk black Ceylons, or other black tea blends to rev up the physical body and engage in classes or work that require clear-headed, focused thinking. The orange blossom signals "your purity is equal to your loveliness." It also means pure generosity, surely a wonderful attitude when facing challenge or adversity in love or career. Besides, it just makes one feel good to be surrounded by happy "orangeness."

## CHERRY

A traditional ingredient in Japanese green teas, the cherry is not unlike what it appears: round and red like the blood of life, sweet and delicious yet with a hard pit that must be removed for ease in eating. The delicate aroma of the cherry blossom sends out the "spirit of beauty" every time it is used. A rather prosaic Victorian definition is that of "a good education"; however, I prefer to think of the glorious sight of cherry blossoms in spring, their pink-white leaves filling the air with delicate fragrance, the tree's branches laden with beauty.

## CHRYSANTHEMUM

Although not used for fragrance as much as for taste, chrysanthemum petals are a popular complement to Chinese teas, and used to make a tisane. When the pale yellow petals are infused with the tea liquor, they blossom into peony-like shapes. Chrysanthemum adds wonderful flavor to any China black or lightly processed oolong tea.

# Vessels for Tea and Your Spirit

*When you place a tea utensil, you should withdraw your hand*
*as though it were a loved one you were leaving.*

—Rikyû

*S*avoring tea after meditation is a way to extend the bliss following your inner traveling. Contemplating which tea to drink is a pleasure in and of itself, as is choosing which vessels to use in pouring the tea or for drinking. A special cup and pot can be reserved just for this experience, but I should warn you if you are new to tea and meditation, that despite the importance of simplicity, it is hard not to start a collection of beautiful or whimsical or boldly utilitarian cups.

## Teacups

IF YOU DON'T KNOW where to begin, start with a plain white cup that will show off the tea's color vividly. Its serene simplicity will do much to contribute to your overall experience. If this cup satisfies, by all means use it each time you surrender to the meditation experience.

Style, shape, and color of teacups are legion; the teacup is a favored form for potters and designers and to say there are thousands of designs is probably an understatement. Handles are a relatively new idea. Oriental teacups, used in China, Korea, Japan, and other countries throughout the Pacific Rim, have no handles. The idea is that if a cup is too hot to hold, its liquid will be too hot to drink. These cups are small, generally holding two to three ounces, so when someone suggests one or two cups of tea, the actual quantity consumed is not much.

By comparison, European teacups hold five ounces (coffee cups hold six). Mugs hold anywhere from six to twelve ounces, and sometimes more. (This is why your coffee percolator, marked to make ten cups, seems to make only six!)

European cups were originally handleless and featured a saucer that matched. Some tea drinkers poured tea from the cup into the saucer and drank it that way; others used the saucer to stand the cup upon when not in use. Soon, British and French potters were attaching handles to teacups (along with legs and curves and exquisitely detailed scenes).

To retain heat best, cups should be made of porcelain or the fine Chinese clay called *yixing*. Cups can be opaque or translucent for visual splendor; solid, sturdy crockery; or many grades in between. They can be colorful or pale, decorated or plain, round or cylindrical or even square. They can be perfectly executed or, in the Japanese tradition of *wabi-sabi*, have a slight imperfection that makes an object doubly appealing. You do indeed have choices, and having several cups does allow you the opportunity to choose a cup to suit your mood or the day.

145

# Yixing Ware

YIXING TEAPOTS and cups are a special category. Produced for nearly five hundred years, the pots come in both severely plain and outrageously ornate designs. One important feature of this clay is that pots and cups fashioned from it not only retain heat superbly, but will, after time, retain the flavor of the tea brewed inside them. This is because neither the inside nor the outside of the vessel is glazed. When purchasing a Yixing teapot, you must dedicate it for brewing only one type of tea, such as a Dragonwell or a Sencha; a Keemun or an Assam; a Ti Kwan Yin or a Formosa Oolong. Legend has it that in ten to twenty years, you will be able to fill the pot with hot water and have a flavorful cup without first adding any tea.

# Gung Fu Sets

*Gung fu* sets are particular to Taiwan and its charming tea ceremony that calls for very small pots and tiny cups, often referred to as thimble cups, although they're much larger than a standard thimble. The pots are generally used for brewing large-leafed oolong teas, which, when placed in these pots, produce a tea with an intense concentrated flavor. It is fully decanted with each infusion. These sets can, of course, be used to prepare and serve any kind of tea, but it is recommended that each pot be used repeatedly for the same type of tea, as described above for the Yixing pots.

# Guywan

THIS THREE-PIECE cup set is a masterful example of form and function. The curvaceous cup allows the tea leaves to unfurl, the coaster is used to set the cup onto a table, and the lid is the most ingenious part of all. It is a lid to assist brewing, and it is also a paddle, to push the leaves to and fro so that they can completely offer up their nectar. It is a cup to drink from, and it also is a vessel to pour tea from into a small cup or two.

# Teapots and Filters

To MAKE TEA, one only needs the tea, hot water, and a vessel to brew the tea in. Quality teas will sink to the bottom when brewed so that you can sip from the cup with no need for a filter or strainer. A food strainer, with a round mesh bowl on one end and a handle at the other, makes a perfect tea strainer. Brew tea in one cup, pour it through the strainer into a second up, and *voila!*, you have a cup of tea.

Aluminum, brass, and other metals do not make good teapots. Some people use them for containing hot water, but they do give off a metallic taste. Stainless steel does not affect the taste of water. Cast-iron pots (*tesubin*) are a Japanese classic, but to make clean-tasting tea use one with a glazed enamel interior. The best pot for brewing is clay, either the unglazed Yixing ware or the glazed clay from England that makes the "Brown Betty" pot. Second is any porcelain teapot. All of these effectively retain heat, give off no odors, and are available almost everywhere.

Teapots are round for a reason; so that the leaves can float and whirl and infuse the water with flavor. Some come with filters in the spout. For your solo tea pleasures, buy small pots so that you can completely decant the tea into a cup. It is far better to empty the pot and pour hot water on the leaves each time you want another cup. If you want to brew the tea all at once, then place the tea leaves in a filter, put the filter in the pot, pour on the hot water, and when the tea is brewed, remove the filter and set it aside. This way, the tea remains hot in the pot, so to speak, and does not continue to brew.

Filters or strainers make for neat presentation but they are not necessary when using good-quality tea because the leaves naturally fall to the bottom of the cup or teapot. However, if you cannot resist, purchase filters that are mesh fabric or gold, or made of porcelain or stainless steel with evenly sized holes. Filters can also be made of unbleached paper, or cotton cloth "socks" work very well. The paper ones are easy to use and totally disposable. The socks stain over time, but they are very reliable when timing the tea and the tea does not take on any taste from the material. Plastic mesh filters work fine, but the poorly made ones stain badly, tear, and sometimes give off a plastic taste to the tea. Forget those cute little tea balls and tea spoons with clip-on bowls to hold tea; they do not allow the leaves to fully infuse. And, attractive though they may be, avoid silverplate strainers, which frequently oxidize or wear to expose the brass underneath. And don't use brass or aluminum strainers either. They are sure to give a metallic taste to your tea. If you can't resist the variety and charm of their looks, buy them and keep them in your collection, but do not use them for the preparation of tea.

As you become adventurous with your tea choices, you will discover that less is enormously satisfying. Quantity is irrelevant. A three-ounce cup of very fine tea is infinitely more fulfilling than a quart thermos of mediocre tea. Fine tea offers a floral bouquet, delicate to intense flavor, and painterly color. It does quench our thirst, but it also does something greater—it gratifies the spirit. Tea, my dear readers, *is* meditation. ☙

# RESOURCES

*What's this, Aurora Leigh,*
*You write so of the poets, and not laugh?*
*Those virtuous liars, dreamers after dark,*
*Exaggerators of the sun and moon,*
*And soothsayers in a tea-cup?*

—Elizabeth Barrett Browning (1806–1861)

## Exceptional Tea Experiences

THE FOLLOWING are either sources for teas or tea shops that offer something truly unusual for the meditative tea experience. These are not your typical, or atypical, English afternoon tea salons, but rather tea sources dedicated to the pure singular pleasure of fine, even rare, teas.

## Dushanbe Tea House

1770 Thirteenth Street
Boulder, Colorado 80302
303-442-4993
www.boulderteahouse.com

In 1990, this Russian-style tearoom, with elaborate ceramic and wooden detailing, opened in Boulder, a testament to the sister city relationship between Boulder and Dushanbe, a city in the Russian province of Tajikstan. Dushanbe (which means "Monday") Teahouse offers a popular tea festival in the summer and classes throughout the year where one can learn about tea ceremonies from a variety of cultures. Afternoon tea is served, and the teas and teapots offered at the teahouse and online also reflect the style and quality of the various ceremonies celebrated there. The building is unlike anything you can imagine, full of beauty and whimsy, elegance and charm.

## Elixir Tonics & Teas

8612 Melrose Ave.
Los Angeles, California 90069-5011
310-657-9300
www.elixir.net

In the heart of designer row, in the shadow of architectural oddities and individualism on steroids, is this corridor of comfort and serenity. The front space is devoted to their inventory of excellent teas and beautiful accessories, and their tonics and elixirs, hence the name. What draws the city's movers and shakers is the garden in the rear, dotted with tables and chairs not-so subtlety spaced far from each other to allow each patron the time, and space, to savor tea in peace amidst the lush plantings. An inviting L.A. anachronism.

## Franchia

12 Park Avenue
New York, New York 10016-4307
212-213-1001
www.franchia.com

This oasis of serenity puts a delicate light on rare Korean teas and offers visitors an arresting inventory of teas and accessories, informative classes, and a genuinely serene experience for dining and drinking tea. A welcomed respite.

## Imperial Tea Court

1411 Powell Street
San Francisco, California 94133-3803
415-788-6080 *or* 800-567-5898
www.imperialteas.com

Still the only authentic Chinese teahouse in the United States, Imperial Tea Court has been instrumental in elevating awareness of the conviviality and pure joy of Chinese tea drinking in the city of San Francisco and to thousands of customers visiting from around the country and around the world. Patrons have relaxed at glossy rosewood tables in the beautifully appointed room decorated with fine silk fabric walls and classic one-piece lanterns overhead casting a soft glow. On Saturdays, the sweet tweet-tweet of caged finches is pure entertainment. Of course, the real reason to visit is the tea, and now their superb tea from aged pu-erhs to the rarest whites, and their exquisite Yixing teapots are available to all online. When in San Francisco, stop in for Chinese tea at its simplest and best. Second location in the Ferry Building on the Embarcadero (415-544-9830).

## The Peaceful Dragon Tea House
12610 Steele Creek Rd.
Charlotte, North Carolina 28273-3770
704-504-8866
www.thepeacefuldragon.com

A combination of everything Asian from fine teas and accessories to lectures, meditation, and martial arts classes, and everything you need to get the most out of each event they offer. A genuine gem of a concept realized.

## The Tea Box at Takashimaya
693 Fifth Avenue
New York, New York 10017-1913
800-753-2038, ext. 8

In the basement of this Japanese shop is a ubiquitous spot of serenity in the heart of the madness of Manhattan. Menu selections for this unusual tea room change frequently; however everything is graciously presented with beauty and wit, and the teas are superb. Teas and accessories for sale.

## Tea Garden Springs

38 Miller Avenue
Mill Valley, California 94941
415-389-7123
www.teagardensprings.com

Before and after your relaxing massage, you will be feted with an exquisitely prepared cup of tea from beautiful cups and pots. Everything from the teas and accessories to the incense, books, and massage products has been chosen with an eye to your comfort and pleasure. The masseuses are angels, the experience divine.

## Teaism

2009 R Street NW
Washington, D.C. 20009-1011
202-667-3827

800 Connecticut Avenue NW
Washington, D.C. 2006
202-835-2233

400 Eighth Street NW
Washington, DC 20094
202-638-6010

What if you created a restaurant dedicated to eating and drinking tea? This spot has proved so popular, it now has three branches in the nation's capital city. The place for excellent classes, tea tastings, and a restful place to enjoy tea and foods made with tea.

## *LuLu's Tealuxe*

Zero Battle Street Harvard Square
Cambridge, Massachusetts 02138
617-441-0077 *or* 888-TEALUXE [832-5893]
www.tealuxe.com

231 Thayer St.
Providence, Rhode Island 02906-1215
401-453-4832

108 Newbury St.,
Boston, Massachusetts 02116-2904
617-927-0400

*For other locations call 617-244-3155*

If *Cheers* had served tea instead of alcohol, it would be called Tealuxe, a tea bar in the most charming sense of the phrase. The Cambridge shop is now a Harvard community landmark, and the two spin-offs in Providence and Boston, and a web site give those outside Cambridge easy access to great teas, good solid information, and a nice choice of accessories.

> *The muse has to know where to find you.*
>
> —Attributed to Billy Wilder (1910–2003),
> screenwriter and director

# Web Sites and Mail Order Sources for Tea

THESE ONLINE SOURCES provide excellent, sometimes superb, teas that I highly recommend not only for their delicious taste and fragrance, but also for the experience of trying something unusual and out of the ordinary. Buy in small quantities for freshness and use up during a few weeks to two months after purchase for best flavor. You will note that most provide online buying services, although a few have avoided cyberspace completely except for email. High-quality teabag sources have been included for those too reticent to go for the gold . . . just yet . . . in the packaged tea list shown on page 165.

## www.acornplanet.com

Primarily a site for inkstone and handmade Chinese paper, it nonetheless offers a very few but exquisite selections of rare teas like Mao Feng for the discriminating palate as well as fascinating Yixing (Zisha) teaware. Very limited supplies but worth the wait and the price.

## Adagio Teas
877-ADAGIO-T [232-4468]
www.discovertea.com

Adagio Teas, which literally and figuratively offer you music to drink, are well priced, the accessories are either whimsical or elegant, and their directions make brewing easy, easy, easy. Try the sample packs if the decisions look overwhelming. Lively site with lots of information and lots of great tea choices that you can order 24 hours a day.

## devotea
888-832-6505
www.devotea.com

Elegant combination of superb teas, glamorous tabletop furnishings, and classic packaged teas from Ashby's and Typhoo. Fun to browse.

## Freeds
800-370-7371
www.freedscoffeetea.com

Since 1899, the carriage trade of San Francisco has depended upon this company for excellent teas (and coffees), but when it closed its shop and opened up in cyberspace, it was the beginning of serving a wider audience than previously imaginable. Offers at least ninety fine teas, the Lindsay's packaged lines, the Swiss gold filter, Brown Betty teapot, and many other accessories and tea-related products. Personal service at no extra charge.

## Holy Mountain Trading Co.
888-832-8008
www.holymtn.com

Chatty, informative site with lovely and distinctly different handmade tea accessories and both classic and exotic teas from Vietnam's Chi Tsi Beengcha to the finest Chinese Pi Lo Chun. Lots to read and explore about tea and good choices for accessories both conventional and unusual.

## In Pursuit of Tea
866-878-3832
www.inpursuitoftea.com

The owners balance a wanderlust for exotic traveling with offerings of true teas that are as beautiful and delicious as they are unusual—like a Thailand oolong or a Silver Needle or a *pu-erh*. The classics are readily available, along with very discriminating sampler packs for those who'd like to try several teas for one modest price. Nice selection of accessories, too.

## www.japanesegreenteaonline.com

It is true, my personal passion of late is for Japanese green teas, and the *fukimatcha*, several choices of *matcha*, and the *genmaicha* with a dollop of *matcha* available at this site are fantastic. These are, literally, direct from the farm to you. A trifle expensive, and definitely worth it each delicious sip.

## Red Crane Teas
303-477-3642
www.redcraneteas.com

Limited but excellent selection of the finest teas in the world provided by those who live, breathe, and drink tea.

### Rishi Teas

866-747-4483

www.rishi-tea.com

Very selective offerings of both teas and accessories, and dedicated to selling only the best, with specific suggestions for water that best brings out the flavor profiles of their teas. Wonderful oolongs and *pu-erhs* are among their list of teas, and the list grows as veteran "nose" Joshua Kaiser seeks out only the best of each season. Elegant canisters and teapots and clever filters.

### Shan Shui Teas

202-483-2836

www.shanshuiteas.com

This is the place for the sweet nectar of Korean green teas, plus Chinese *pu-erhs* and premier oolongs from Taiwan. Limited, carefully selected choices of superb teas and wonderful accessories. *Shan Shui* means "mountains and water," the two geographical ingredients to superb teas.

### Silk Road Teas

P.O. Box 10

Lagunitas, California 94938

415-488-9017

These are the teas for the purist, the thrill-seeking, and the curious. Some of the finest Chinese tea available, they are chosen and packaged with intelligence and care. David Lee Hoffman doesn't only buy the teas himself on numerous visits to China. He is also an active participant in the planting, growing, and harvesting of teas, using his extensive knowledge of vermiculture, nearly thirty years of tea-tasting, and travels and tea tasting experiences throughout the world.

## SpecialTeas, Inc.
888-365-6983
www.specialteas.com

Excellent, consistent variety of fine teas from around the world and good general choice of accessories for the enjoyment of every type and style of tea. Chosen with care and sensibility.

## Teas of Green
888-977-4800
www.teasofgreen.com

Superb site that's elegantly designed with a limited but well-chosen line of greens, oolongs, and blacks, and exquisite teaware for a lush drinking experience.

## teavana
877-374-6583
www.teavana.com

Chain of stores in Georgia, Minnesota, Nevada, Virginia, and Florida, with something for everyone, from Chun Mei to Citrus Green Earl Grey or Kenya

Marinyn to Keemun among their 100-plus selection. Lots of cast-iron Japanese teapots (*tesubin*) and Chinese Yixing pots, too.

### Thompson's Fine Teas
800-830-8835
www.fineteas.com

Simple, direct, no-nonsense site for good-quality teas and excellent accessories. Good value for the dollar, especially their tea club specials.

### Upton Tea Imports
800-234-8327
www.uptontea.com

Broad-range inventory of excellent teas and accessories from around the world with something wonderful for every taste. For almost fifteen years, the source for teas chosen with enthusiasm for the leaf.

> *Silence is not a thing we make; it is something into which we enter.*
>
> —Maribel, Mother Superior (1882–1970)

# Packaged Teas

THESE ARE AMONG the top packaged teas available on the market. Most offer selections in loose leaf and some tea bags, often made with high-quality pouches or fine paper bags. These are economical, accessible ways to try a variety of teas and help you educate yourself to your personal tastes. Then you'll be ready to visit a tea shop and experience loose leaf tea by the ounce in choices far beyond anything on your grocer's shelf.

## Barnes and Watson

206-625-9435

www.barnesandwatson.com

Excellent source for a wide variety of hot and cold teas, including kosher teas. Fine-quality accessories, too.

## Choice Organic Teas/Granum, Inc.

206-525-0051

www.choiceorganicteas.com

This company has dedicated itself to the purity and quality of the finest organic teas from around the world, many of them Fair Trade teas, those with the extra mission of assisting the laborers who work so tirelessly to plant, pluck, and package teas. The company goes beyond the philosophical, however, and provides top-grade teas in convenient packaged form. Available wherever fine foods are sold, from Whole Foods to upscale markets.

### Golden Moon Tea, Ltd.
425-820-2000

www.goldenmoontea.com

A superb packaged line of tea with many rare, limited reserve teas not found anywhere else. Worth every penny. Available via mail order and from some upscale grocers.

### Grace Tea Company, Ltd.
212-255-2935

www.graceraretea.com

Limited choices, but each of the highest quality.

### Harney & Sons Fine Tea
888-427-6398

www.harney.com

This family-run firm offers a tea or accessory for every taste and every pocketbook. Be sure to read about Michael's picks on the web site, rare or unusual teas sure to tempt your palate. When in Salisbury, Connecticut, visit the Harney tea tasting room for information and great tea sipping.

### Honest Tea
800-865-4736 *or* 301-652-3556

www.honesttea.com

Charming selection of bottled teas including the first Fair Trade oolong bottled tea, Peach Oo-la-long. Growing line of high-quality teabag selections.

Great for taking along with you to the office, shopping, traveling, or just hanging out on the veranda. This is a company with a conscience and great style.

### Leaves Pure Leaves
877-532-8378
www.leaves.com

Simplicity. Style. Sensuous. A less-is-more attitude toward the delicacy of tea and its ability to heal, nourish, and satisfy. Beautifully practical accessories and limited but elegant selection of teas on this site. The drip teapot is a terrific idea for one-step brewing. Great care for healthful teas is part of their mission, and it shows.

### Lindsay's Teas
800-624-7031
www.mountanosbros.com/shop00b.htm

Mountanos Brothers, a pioneer coffee company, created this excellent line of organic and nonorganic teas and tisanes. Excellent quality and easy-to-store round tins.

### Mighty Leaf
877-698-5323
www.mightyleaf.com *or* www.mltea.com

This fun site offers both loose-leaf teas and an exceptional pouch-style tea bag of full leaves that makes tea drinking appealing to those both new to and experienced in tea. Lots of fascinating blends, good advice, and small select group of accessories.

### Numi Teas and Teasans

510-567-8903

www.numitea.com

Award-winning packaged tea with good quality and carefully chosen accessories.

### Percival Boyd's Teas of Origins

800-223-8211

www.boyds.com

Limited yet exceptional selection of "can't-miss" teas.

### The Republic of Tea

800-298-4TEA[4832]

www.republicoftea.com

The originator of marketing the mind-conscious quality of tea to the general audience, the company now offers everything from bottled teas to travel packs of round tea bags for quick hops around the world. Best choices are new certified organic teas and limited rare selections showcased seasonally.

## Royal Gardens Tea

800-648-6491

www.royalgardenstea.com

This is a company with a conscience and a considerably informed palate, that offers a limited but excellent inventory of fine quality tea in bags; many are certified organic, and all are flavorful and well priced.

## serendipitea

888-832-5433

www.serendipitea.com

Limited yet interesting selection of quality accessories teas, including a Jasmine Apple Green and Vanilla Black Orchid Tea that benefits City Harvest, New York's food rescue organization.

## Simpson & Vail

800-282-8327

www.svtea.com

Good selection of quality teas, accessories, and everything for the English afternoon enthusiast. They've been selling teas for novices and connoisseurs since the carriage trade days when they created a signature blend for financier J. P. Morgan.

## Stash Teas
800-800-TEAS[8327]
www.stashtea.com

Skip over the usual and head straight to their premier lines that offer organic, limited, estate selections and excellent fine loose leaf teas and quality teabag selections. Plus, every book, accessory, and tschotske you can imagine—from tea incense to tea bricks. A fun and entertaining site.

## Mark T. Wendell Tea Company
978-369-3709
www.marktwendell.com

Carries classic and rare tea brands including Foojoy selections of Pi Lo Chun, Silvertip White, Imperial Keemun, Lung Ching, Sichuan Meng Ding Green, Huang Mountain Mao Feng Green, jasmines, oolongs, and many others, including the infamous Hu-kwa Lapsang souchong.

> *The pot is the father of tea,*
> *Water is the mother of tea,*
> *And charcoal is the friend of tea.*
>
> —Traditional Japanese saying

# Yixing Teapots

World Treasure Trading Co.
815 Piner Road
Santa Rosa, California 95403-2020
707-566-7888

Premier importing firm for tea caddies, teapots, and other Yixing ware that is guaranteed lead-free and excellent for traditional Chinese tea making. Choose from the whimsical, the elegant, and the purely functional. Wholesale and retail.

> *With an eye made quiet by the power*
> *Of harmony, and the deep power of joy,*
> *We see into the life of things.*
>
> —William Wordsworth (1770–1850)

# Stellar Tea Shops and Tea Rooms

No single list can include all of the many tea rooms and tea shops in the U.S. These are just a few. I encourage you to try these and new ones in your area as part of "Tea Fun."

## Bamboo Tea House

700 E. Colorado Boulevard
Pasadena, California 91101-2102
626-577-0707
  or
221 Yale Avenue
Claremont, California 91711-4725
909-626-7668
www.bambooteas.com

A restful invitation to shop online for loads of accessories and excellent teas, or stop by the pretty little shops and see the many delights of gung fu accessories and sample a fragrant oolong as it was meant to be tasted.

## Chado Tea Rooms

8422½ W. Third Street
Los Angeles, California 90048-4112
800-442-4019
  also
79 N. Raymond Avenue
Pasadena, California 91103-3919
626-431-2832
www.chadotea.com

Restful, charming tea rooms that bespeak a contemporary elegance. Terrific food, many made with tea, and a mind-numbing selection of 250-plus teas. Owner Devan Shah has a superb "nose" for blending and buying. Excellent source for both whimsical and traditional tea accessories.

## Corti Brothers

5810 Folsom Boulevard
Sacramento, California 95819-4610
916-736-3800

Eclectic market focuses on fine wine and an unusually interesting group of fine Chinese teas that change with the seasons. Print newsletter available.

## The Cultured Cup

5346 Belt Line Road
Dallas, Texas 75254-7682
972-960-1521
www.theculturedcup.com

It's not all sweet tea in Texas. This clean and neat, fully-stocked shop offers everything from tea tastings and afternoon tea classes, plus teas, teaware and tea table accessories.

## Guy's Tea/Empire Tea Services

5155 Hartford Avenue
Columbus, Indiana 47203-4117
812-375-1937 or 800-790-0246
www.guystea.com

A manager for decades on Sri Lanka tea farms, the owner now runs a great tea room and full-service tea company offering excellent choices for afternoon tea aficionados right in the heart of the United States.

## Herbal Republic™

2680 W. Broadway
Vancouver, Canada, V6K 2G3
604-732-1732
www.herbalrepublic.com

This Vancouver-based firm is dedicated to both the pleasure of fine teas and of trying new things. Excellent choices of teas from around the world, particularly Taiwan and Japan, and lots of beautiful accessories you will not find anywhere else. Their mission is to offer both teas and accessories that are authentic in style and content, and you will not be disappointed. Drop by their shop and get a personal tea tasting.

## House of Tea, Ltd.

720 South Fourth Street
Philadelphia, Pennsylvania 19147
888-923-8327
www.houseoftea.com

Founded by the late Nat Litt, this shop has become the spot for fine teas and accessories in the city of brotherly love. They carry Lomonosov Russian cups, British Chatsford pots, and an impressive and extensive list of teas for every taste and budget.

## Le Palais des Thés

401 North Canon Drive
Beverley Hills, California 90210
310-271-7922
www.palaisdesthes.com

The bright red awnings signal a fresh invitation to this sophisticated, clean-lined shop and small corner tea bar. Everything is *"très français,"* from the scented soaps and candles to the intelligent and sensitive selection of well-priced teas and accessories aimed at appealing to all of the senses.

## Perennial Tea Room

1910 Post Alley
Seattle, Washington 98101-1015
888-448-4054
www.perennialtearoom.com

Located on one of Seattle's hidden treasure streets, this tiny shop is full of elegant and whimsical teapots and a nice selection of good quality teas and accessories.

## Silver Tips Tea Room

3 North Broadway
Tarrytown, New York 10591-3201
866-TEA-4245 [832-4245]
www.silvertipstea.com

Operated by one of our country's premier importers of tea, Silver Tips is the place to go for a wide yet carefully selected inventory of 120 fine teas.

Scrumptious food, great events, and exceptional organic teas, including the highly-prized Mak'aibari Darjeeling.

### La Société du Thé

2708 Lyndale Avenue South
Minneapolis, Minnesota 55408-1301
888-871-5148
www.la-societe-du-the.com

With a decidedly French twist in form and function, this wonderful shop offers a very fresh assortment of teas, pots and cups, and other teatime delights for both European and Oriental tea pleasures, including Mariage Frères. They do their utmost to follow the French maxim: "On n'existe que pour servir les feuilles"—one only exists to serve the leaves.

### Tao of Tea

3430 SE Belmont St.
Portland, Oregon 97214-4247
503-736-0198
www.taooftea.com

Eclectic, charming, and great spot for tea; also provides excellent teas served at the teahouse in the Chinese Gardens. They have opened several other locations, including one with a Japanese tea room at 2112 NW Hoyt Street.

## The Tea House

541 Fessler Avenue
Naperville, Illinois 60565-1215
630-961-0877
www.theteahouse.com

Exceptional selections of Chinese teas and blended-to-order teas are the specialty here, but whatever classic teas and accessories you desire you'll find here, too. American owner, speaks Mandarin and English, and conducts tours of tea farms in China. Call for details.

## Tea Rex® Tearoom

2102 South Blvd. #150
Charlotte, North Carolina 28203-5004
704-371-4440
www.tearex.com

Wayne Powers is a successful actor, comedian, and jazz artist. When he couldn't find a good cup of tea in town, he opened his own tea bar—and a new "act" of his life. Located in Charlotte's historic district, it's a charming tea shop where people can hang out and enjoy the world's finest teas and gifts, or take them home. Happy ending.

## The Tea Room

7 E. Broughton Street
Savannah, Georgia 31401-3301
912-239-9690
www.savannahtearoom.com

Among the whispering trees sits this shop with a quirky combination: design as an homage to Charles Rennie Mackintosh, food that satisfies, and tea with a twist. Excellent, excellent, excellent.

## Tea Source

752 Cleveland Avenue South
St. Paul, Minnesota 55116-1347
651-690-9822
www.teasource.com
Informed source of tea with excellent selection of teas and tea ware.

## Ten Ren Tea and Ginseng Company

650-583-1044 or 877-898-0858
www.tenren.com

For over four decades, this family-run company has been the premier Taiwanese source of oolong teas and *gung fu* accessories, along with exceptional *pu-erhs* and greens from Mainland China. Most shops have a *gung fu* demonstration table in the rear. More than twenty locations in northern and southern California, Houston, Baltimore, Chicago, and New York.

## Todd & Holland Tea Merchants

7577 Lake Street
River Forest, Illinois 60305-1846
800-747-8327
www.todd-holland.com

Wood-paneled, relaxed shop with everything you need and much of what we all want in the way of exceptional teas and excellent accessories. Good expertise on the website, too.

## Two for the Pot

200 Clinton Street
Brooklyn, New York 11201
718-855-8173

This coffee, tea, and spice company offers a plethora of outstanding British tea brand names and Ireland's Barry's, Bewley's, Lyons, and McGrath's; Japan's oldest line, Yamamotoyama, and China's Foojoy Brand of rare teas. Extensive selection of bulk teas and tins from India, China, Japan, Kenya, and American Classic Tea. Also offers custom blends, including their signature Earl Grey.

*Always remember to bound thy thoughts to the present occasion.*

—William Penn

# Learning More About Chanoyu

THE FOLLOWING are the main foundation centers for the study of Japanese tea ceremony. Most can provide names and sources for teachers in your area.

**Japan**

Kyoto: Headquarters for Urasenke Konnichian, Ogawa Teranouchi Dori agaru, Kamikyo-ku, Kyoto, 602 Japan

**Canada**

British Columbia: Stages classes at university locations in Vancouver and at its Coquitlam headquarters. For details, call 604-224-1560.

**United States**

chadosf@aol.com or www.urasenke.org

California: 2143 Powell St, San Francisco, CA 94133; 415-433-6553

Hawaii: 245 Saratoga Rd., Honolulu, HI 96815; 808-923-1057 urasenke@lava.net

New York: 153 E. 69th St., New York, NY 10021; 212-988-6161 urasenke@earthlink.net

Virginia: 6930 Hector Rd., McLean, VA 22101; 703-748-1685. Private classes only. (All others listed are open to the public.)

Washington: 1910 37th Pl. E., Seattle, WA 98112; 206-324-1483 urasenkeseattle@hotmail.com or www.urasenkeseattle.org

# Learning More About Labyrinths

Veriditas™: The World-Wide Labyrinth Project
Grace Cathedral
1100 California Street
San Francisco CA 94108
415-749-6358
TTY: 415-749-6359
www.gracecathedral.org/labyrinth/index.shtml

The pioneer of the labyrinth movement in the U.S., The Rev. Dr. Lauren Artress, is a canon at San Francisco's Grace Cathedral and the founder of Veriditas™, the organization that has been most instrumental in promoting the labyrinth as a tool for spiritual awareness here in this country. She is the author of *Walking a Sacred Path: Rediscovering the Labyrinth as a Spiritual Tool*, Putnam/Riverhead Books, 1996.

## Adrian Fisher Mazes Ltd.

Portman Lodge, Durweston, Blandford Forum
Dorset DT11 0QA England
011-44 (0)12 58 458845
For U.S. contact, please call: 702-733-7722
www.maze-world.com/usapavlab.htm

Fisher is a designer and builder of labyrinths around the world, and his very extensive site lists labyrinths, both Christian and non-Christian, throughout the world.

# Learning More About Tea

Rosen, Diana. *The Book of Green Tea*. Boston: Storey Books, 1999.

Okakura, Kakuzo. *The Book of Tea*. New York: Dover Publications, Inc., 1972.

Sadler, A.L. *Cha-no-yu: The Japanese Tea Ceremony*. Boston: Charles E. Tuttle, Co., 1977.

Yu, Lu, 1780, translated by Francis Ross Carpenter. *The Classic of Tea, Origins & Rituals*. New York: Ecco Press, 1996.

Tanaka, Sen-o. *The Tea Ceremony*. Tokyo: Kodansha International, Ltd., 1973.

Sôshitsu, XV, Sen. *Tea Life, Tea Mind*. Boston: Charles E. Tuttle Co., 1979.

Master Lam Kam Chuen with Lam Kai Sin and Lam Tin Yu, *The Way of Tea, The Sublime Art of Oriental Tea Drinking*. New York: Gaia Books Ltd., dba Barron's Educational Series, 2002.

# Learning More About Meditation

KABBALAH, BUDDHISM, Taoism, Transcendental Meditation, yoga breathing, prayer and religious ceremonies for all religions, and "just sitting" or "just walking" are all tools with tremendous power to comfort, energize, empower, and liberate. Browse your local library, bookshop, or the gift shop attached to your church, synagogue, temple, or mosque. You are sure to find books, audiotapes, and videotapes that will help you learn more, go deeper, become more accomplished with techniques for meditation. With experience, you will discover which techniques suit you best, satisfy your longing for serenity, and strengthen your desire to live more fully. Take a class. Attend a lecture. Read. Experiment. Nurture the solace of silence, prayer, meditation, deep breathing. May these explorations keep you on the path to inner peace all your life.

# ENDNOTES

OTHER WRITERS, POETS, and essayists are a constant inspiration for my personal meditations, offering wisdom and wit as guides for my own life path. Therefore, I have sprinkled *Meditations with Tea* with many of my favorite quotes on meditation, inspiration, dreams, and of course, tea. Although these endnotes are listed to satisfy curiosity, I encourage you to explore any and all of these authors more fully, and to keep a meditation journal just for jotting down any words or phrases that affect you deeply. Reading them at the beginning or end of your own meditations with tea is another way to deepen your experience.

**PAGE xiv**
Eda LeShan was a family counselor, columnist of "Life After Sixty" and author of many books, including *It's Better to be Over the Hill than Under It*. Newmarket Press, 1997.

**PAGE xvi**
George Herbert was a British poet and minister who wrote many liturgical and philosophical texts, and poems, including "The Church-Porch," which includes this stanza.

**PAGE 1**

Marcus Aurelius was a Roman emperor and philosopher famous for his daily meditations that reflected his stoic philosophy. They were gathered into the book *Meditations*, from which this quote is derived. It is iv23.

**PAGE 2**

Ezra Pound was an American poet and critic. This quote is from a letter to his wife, Dorothy Shakespear, who was his fiancée at the time. It appears in *Ezra Pound and Dorothy Shakespear: Their Letters 1909–1914*, eds. Omar Pound and A. Walton Litz, 1985.

**PAGE 3**

Robert Louis Stevenson was a Scottish novelist, essayist, and poet for adults and children. This quote comes from "A Night Among the Pines" from *Travels with a Donkey*, published in 1879.

**PAGE 4**

Victor Hugo was a prolific French novelist whose most popular work is *Les Misérables*.

**PAGE 6**

Lines 1 through 9 from Paul Hookham's poem, "A Meditation," published in *The Oxford Book of English Mystical Verse*, 1917, Nicholson & Lee, eds.

Henry David Thoreau was an American essayist. This line is from the Conclusion to his seminal work, *Walden*.

**PAGE 12**

Sen no Rikyû was the sixteenth-century Tea Master who was instrumental in formalizing the ritual of tea in Japan. He was also a poet and sage, and earned the patronage and respect of the shogun Hideyoshi, who after decades of support became displeased with Rikyû. Rikyû committed suicide for inferred sins against his patron. Rikyû's writings about the simplicity of tea, the critical elements of harmony and beauty within the teahouse, and the engagement of guests with host remain the ultimate guide for the followers of *chanoyu*, "water for tea."

**PAGE 14**

From chapter 1 of *Moby-Dick*, published originally in 1851, by American author Herman Melville.

**PAGE 16**

The Czech novelist and short story writer Franz Kafka wrote many pithy sayings, some collected in "The Collected Aphorisms," vol. 1, no. 109, *Shorter Works*, edited and translated by Malcolm Pasley, 1973.

**PAGE 21**

Rev. Sydney Smith was an English clergyman and writer whose famous quote used here originally appeared in his book, *Lady Holland's Memoir*, vol.1, page 383.

**PAGE 27**

William Penn, sometimes called the founder of Pennsylvania, wrote a charming treatise, *Advice to His Children*, in which he listed his views on the world, family, and community. This is from Chapter 2, no. 27.

**PAGE 29**

Carl Gustav Jung was a Swiss psychiatrist whose work furthered the interest in the interpretation of dreams through symbols as a gateway to understanding the subconscious.

**PAGE 31**

Mary E. Wilkins Freeman was an early American feminist writer. This quote is from her best-known short story, "A New England Nun," published in 1887.

**PAGE 33**

Matsuo Bashó remains one of the most revered poets of Japanese haiku.

**PAGE 36**

Thich Nhat Hanh is a Vietnamese Zen Buddhist monk now living in France where he lectures and writes. He has written prolifically about peace, meditation, and bringing mindfulness into daily life.

Toyotomi Hideyoshi was a powerful shogun during the sixteenth century, when it was not uncommon for men of his rank to prepare tea as a form of meditation on strength and perseverance prior to going into battle. He was the main patron of tea master Sen no Rikyû.

**PAGE 40**

President Gerald R. Ford gave a speech to the Veterans of Foreign Wars in Chicago on August 19, 1974. This is a quote from his speech, mentioned in reference to Americans who avoided conscription during the Vietnam War.

**PAGE 41**

Aeschylus was an ancient Greek dramatist. This quote is from "Prometheus Unbound: A Lyrical Drama in Four Acts," *Prometheus*, Act I, lines 56–59.

**PAGE 43**

Lorraine Hansberry was the first black woman to have a play produced on Broadway, *A Raisin in the Sun* in 1959.

Joaquin Miller was also known as Cincinnatus Hiner Miller. The stanza quoted is from his poem, "The Voice of the Dove."

**PAGE 44**

David Augsburger is a professor of pastoral care at Fuller Theological Seminary in Pasadena, California, and the author of *Helping People Forgive* and *Caring Enough to Forgive*, from which this quote is derived.

**PAGE 46**

Agnes Repplier was an American author and social critic whose book, *To Think of Tea!*, a paean to the brew, was published in 1932.

**PAGE 48**

Meister Eckhart was a German Catholic Dominican theologian and mystic.

**PAGE 52**

Kakuzo Okakura was a groundbreaking Japanese social critic, art curator, historian, and writer who spent a great deal of time in the United States, and wrote *The Book of Tea*. Published in 1906, it was the first book in English to artfully explain the Japanese way of tea to the Western audience.

**PAGE 54**

Friedrich Kekule was the German chemist who defined the structure of the benzene ring. The unique thing about his solution is that it came from a dream he had in 1865, after fifteen years of working on his theory—truly a demonstration that dreams can help us solve a myriad of problems.

**PAGE 55**

Mowlana Jalal al-Din Rumi was an Afghan poet and philosopher, a practicing Sufi. His enormous body of work is read and admired by legions throughout the world more than nine centuries after his death.

**PAGE 58**

*Meditations*, iv.4, by Marcus Aurelius (see above).

**PAGE 59**

From Erica Jong's "The Artist as Housewife" from *The First Ms. Reader*, edited by Francine Klagsbrun, 1972.

Marcel Proust was a French novelist whose multi-volume autobiographical work, *Remembrance of Things Past* is the source of this quote, from *Nouvelle Revue Francaise*, 1913.

**PAGE 60**

C. S. Lewis was an Irish writer and scholar. This quote is from his autobiography, *Surprised by Joy: The Shape of My Early Life*, pages 115–116, 1955.

**PAGE 63**

William Penn, from Chapter 2, no. 41, *Advice to His Children*.

**PAGE 66**

Last stanza of "Proem," a selection from *Waif* by the American poet and educator Henry Wadsworth Longfellow.

**PAGE 77**

Ken Blanchard is an American motivational speaker and author. This is a quote from his article, "Spirit and Business" from *Entrepreneur* magazine, March, 2000.

**PAGE 81**

Thomas J. Watson was the former chairman and CEO of IBM Corporation

**PAGE 82**

Edmund Waller was an English poet. This stanza is from his poem "Of Tea," in which he pays homage to Lord George Byron's use of "the palace of the soul."

**PAGE 84**

Marianne Moore was an American poet. This line is from "Silence" from her *Selected Poems*, published in 1935.

**PAGE 94**

Lu Yu was the first person to write about tea. His book, *The Classic of Tea, Origins & Rituals*, was first published in his native China in 780 and remains the seminal book about Chinese tea. Lu Yu's text touches on water, leaves, equipment, and attitude that one brings to the enjoyment of tea.

Japanese haiku poet Kobayashi Issa adopted the name Issa ("cup of tea") which is more poetically defined as "a single bubble in steeping tea." He remains hugely popular worldwide.

**PAGE 96**

Rachel Carson was a marine biologist and writer whose books laid the foundation for the awareness of the environment and its tender balance called ecology. This quote is from her book, *Under the Sea-Wind*.

**PAGE 99**

Sen Sôshitsu XV recently turned over the reins as the fifteenth Grand Tea Master of the Urasenke School to his son, following more than five decades of lecturing and traveling around the world offering "a bowl of tea" as a conduit for peace to world leaders. A prolific writer and expert calligrapher, he is best known for *Tea Life, Tea Mind*, a slim treatise on his mission.

**PAGE 103**

D. H. Lawrence was the English-born author of *Sons and Lovers* and many other books and poems. This stanza is from his poem, "Listening," published in *Amores* in 1916.

**PAGE 109**

Paramahansa Yogananda was born Mukunda Lal Ghosh in the state of Bengal, India. He left his life of luxury to become a monk of the Swami Order and founded the Self-Realization Fellowship in 1920 to promote Kriya Yoga.

**PAGE 115**

Ram Dass is an American spiritual leader, prolific writer, and lecturer, formerly known as Richard Alpert, Ph.D., a Harvard-trained psychologist.

**PAGE 153**

Elizabeth Barrett Browning was an English poet; these words are from "Poets," lines 73–77 from *Aurora Leigh*.

**PAGE 164**

Maribel was a sculptor of religious art, and she was Mother Superior from 1940–1953, of the Community of St. Mary the Virgin in Wantage, England.

**PAGE 171**

From "Lines Composed a Few Miles Above Tintern Abbey," 1. 48–50 from *Lyrical Ballads*, published in 1798, by British poet William Wordsworth.

**PAGE 193**

Yuan Mei was an eighteenth-century Chinese poet; this line is from "Tea Drinking."

# ACKNOWLEDGMENTS

WITH THANKS for eagle eyes and insight on the powers of breathing to Iyengar yoga instructor Elizabeth Markley, singer and voice teacher Sandra Leanza, and soprano Gretchen Johnson. Continuous thanks for counsel from tea vendors throughout the world.

Thanks also to the creative touch of cover artist Kristine Noble and interior designer Anne Ricigliano; and to the editorial eyes of Margaret Wolf, Amanda Rouse, and Arthur Maisel.

# THANK YOU

To Joshua Kaiser and Benjamin Harrison of Rishi-Tea for the use of their photographs from their web site, www.rishi-tea.com.

Japanese calligraphy on pages 89–90 is the work of Kankai Onozawa, retired abbot of Jukoin Temple at Daitokuji (Murasakino) in Kyoto, Japan.

Japanese calligraphy on chapter heading pages is the work of master calligrapher Eri Takase, who has earned the rank of Shihan from the Bokuteki-kan calligraphy society in Japan. For more about her work or Takase Studios, please access www.takase.com or write her at eri@takase.com.

*At last, I entered the world of tea . . .*

—Yuan Mei (1716–1798)

# INDEX